Cambridge Elements

Elements in Theatre, Performance and the Political
edited by

CRISIS THEATRE AND THE LIVING NEWSPAPER

Sarah Jane Mullan
BIMM University
Sarah Bartley
Royal Central School of Speech and Drama

CAMBRIDGE
UNIVERSITY PRESS

Shaftesbury Road, Cambridge CB2 8EA, United Kingdom

One Liberty Plaza, 20th Floor, New York, NY 10006, USA

477 Williamstown Road, Port Melbourne, VIC 3207, Australia

314–321, 3rd Floor, Plot 3, Splendor Forum, Jasola District Centre, New Delhi – 110025, India

103 Penang Road, #05–06/07, Visioncrest Commercial, Singapore 238467

Cambridge University Press is part of Cambridge University Press & Assessment, a department of the University of Cambridge.

We share the University's mission to contribute to society through the pursuit of education, learning and research at the highest international levels of excellence.

www.cambridge.org
Information on this title: www.cambridge.org/9781009525794

DOI: 10.1017/9781009525800

When citing this work, please include a reference to the DOI 10.1017/9781009525800

First published 2024

A catalogue record for this publication is available from the British Library.

ISBN 978-1-009-52579-4 Hardback
ISBN 978-1-009-52581-7 Paperback
ISSN 2753-1244 (online)
ISSN 2753-1236 (print)

Crisis Theatre and The Living Newspaper

Elements in Theatre, Performance and the Political

DOI: 10.1017/9781009525800
First published online: March 2024

Sarah Jane Mullan
BIMM University

Sarah Bartley
Royal Central School of Speech and Drama

Author for correspondence: Sarah Bartley, sarah.bartley@cssd.ac.uk

Abstract: *Crisis Theatre and The Living Newspaper* traces a history of the Living Newspaper as a theatre of crisis from Soviet Russia (1910s), through the Federal Theatre Project of the Great Depression in America (1930s), to Augusto Boal's Teatro Jornal in Brazil (1970s), and its resonance with documentary forms deployed in the final years of apartheid in South Africa (1990s), up until the present day in the UK (2020s). Across this Element, the authors are interested in what a transnational and transhistorical examination of the living newspaper through the lens of crisis reveals about the ways in which theatre can intervene in our collective social, economic and political life. By holding these diverse examples together, the authors assert the Living Newspaper as a form of Crisis Theatre.

Keywords: crisis, living newspaper, digital theatre, documentary theatre, theatre histories

ISBNs: 9781009525794 (HB), 9781009525817 (PB), 9781009525800 (OC)
ISSNs: 2753-1244 (online), 2753-1236 (print)

Contents

Introduction: The Front Page

> 'So here we are, together. I don't know how everyone feels about that right now. Some of us might be excited, some of us might be regretting it as the reality settles in. But don't worry, that last one is how a lot of people used to feel at the theatre.
>
> This is Living Newspaper, which makes us living readers. Look around you at all of the other living readers, think about all of the other living readers who can't be here. Think about why they're not. Dumb luck, different choices, fewer opportunities. All three. So, we have been lucky, we have made choices, we have had some opportunities. And we're about to go into this amazing building together. Isn't it great to be alive, mostly. Living readers for a Living Newspaper. Just remember that the people in this building, we don't pretend to know the things that we don't. They just want to start a conversation about what's going on. That's the difference between a Living Newspaper and a dead one, the living version isn't trying to convince us of anything and it can't exist without us being here, so let's go.'
>
> (*Living Newspaper: A Counter Narrative,* Edition One)

Emerging from within the COVID-19 pandemic *Living Newspaper: A Counter Narrative* was commissioned and produced by the Royal Court Theatre in London (UK). In September 2020, the Royal Court Theatre announced they would reopen their building with *Living Newspaper: A Counter Narrative*, describing it as 'A disruption. A manifesto. A celebration'. The project consisted of seven weekly 'editions' produced by over 300 creatives. Each edition brought together a different artistic team of freelance writers, actors, designers, technicians, stage managers, and choreographers to respond to the news of the previous week by theatrically repurposing established newspaper forms including agony aunt letters, the long read, weather forecast, horoscopes, and cartoons. It drew on the 100-year history and political dramaturgy of the Living Newspaper form in different global contexts. As the Royal Court press release announcing the project noted the form is 'a disruptive, responsive, social justice art form for a time of civic and economic trauma' (Royal Court, 2020). The speech at the outset, presented on the outside steps of a theatre in December 2020, opened the first edition of *A Counter Narrative*, with an acknowledgement of the anxiety around collective gathering, an assurance there is no firm message or understanding of what was happening, and a recognition of the living.

In this Element we trace a history of the Living Newspaper from the emergence of the form as its own distinct practice in Soviet Russia (1910s) and wider experimental theatre practices in Europe in the early twentieth century, through the Federal Theatre Project of the Great Depression in the USA (1930s), to Augusto Boal's adaptation of the form in Newspaper Theatre in Brazil (1970s), its utility as part of the documentary performance forms deployed in the final years of apartheid in South Africa (1990s),and its use in the UK to explore the expanding terrain of digital theatre since the turn of the twenty-first century. This form uniquely seeks to critique current events but concurrently asserts the inherent utility of the news to tell stories about who we are, hold individuals accountable, and provoke change. In identifying this set of examples and constructing this particular history of the Living Newspaper, we foreground how the form appears in, speaks to, and is shaped by political, economic, and social crises. We will interrogate how historic and contemporary iterations of the Living Newspaper illuminate material interventions that might be utilised in political performance beyond this specific form (e.g. creating work, promoting inclusive employment, making work accessible to mass audiences). Further, in attending to this form, we address shifts in the sites, consumption, and spectatorship of both news and performance. Finally, we will consider the political potential of responsivity that the form enables asking how this mode responds to the needs of creatives and audiences as well as to the context of its creation.

An explicit engagement with the news media as a core material in, and strategy of, performance making has been traced to the Italian Futurist movement and the experimental theatre movements in Vienna and Germany in the early decades of the twentieth century. John W. Casson illuminates the significance of the experimental theatres of Jacob Levy Moreno's *Das Stegreiftheater* (Theatre of Spontaneity) and the non-naturalistic experiments of Erwin Piscator and Bertold Brecht as germane to the practices that would become key touch points for Living Newspapers (Casson, 2000). The demarcation of the Living Newspaper as a distinct form, with a specific name, has been attributed to Mikhail Pustynin. In Soviet Russia *zhivaia gazeta* – Living Newspapers – were utilised by the Bolsheviks to disseminate information and political messages to the Red Army during the Russian Civil War (1918–1920). Following the end of the war in Russia, the form was popularised by the Blue Blouse Soviet Living Newspaper throughout the 1920s. The Blue Blouses performances sought to engage illiterate workers in the news of the day through: 'skits, verse, monologues, and avant-garde oratory among an uninterrupted montage of scenes, songs, music, dance, mime, acrobatics and gymnastics' (Drain, 2002: 157). However, by the 1930s the popularity and pervasiveness of the form was in decline in Russia, as state support for the revolutionary art form faltered and a turn to social realism was prioritised in cultural policy.

Subsequently, Living Newspapers have appeared in a range of different contexts, regularly in moments of crisis. It was in the 1930s that a variation of the form – *Huobaoju* – began to gain traction in China, where the Chinese Communist Party also deployed it as a propaganda tool during the Second Sino-Japanese War. Jeremy E. Taylor's work on *Huobaoju* depicts the endurance of this practice in China from the 1930s through to the Cultural Revolution

(1966–1976), with it often appearing in periods of war (Chinese Civil War; Korean War), or cultural, economic, and social rupture ('The Great Leap Forward' and the resulting famine). Concurrent to the turn to Living Newspapers in China, the form was also flourishing in the USA and the UK. Indeed, in American theatre histories, the Living Newspaper has become synonymous with the work of the Federal Theatre Project during The Great Depression in 1930s USA. Led by director, playwright, and producer, Hallie Flanagan, the Federal Theatre Project was part of the New Deal, a set of government policies and projects that sought to respond to the collapse of the global stock market collapse of 1929. Living Newspapers became a key tenant of the project, which employed theatre makers (in the case of Living Newspapers, also journalists) across the country to produce performance for a wide range of audiences. Living Newspapers then were a fundamental aspect of one of the largest government investments in culture in American history.

Following these foundational experiments with the Living Newspaper, appetite for the aesthetic and political strategies offered by the form continued to grow in different international contexts, each with contextually specific encounters with social, cultural, and economic rupture. Influenced by the work of theatre makers in the USA – and through visits and correspondence with leaders of the Federal Theatre Project (FTP) – the UK-based Unity Theatre began working with this form in the early 1930s, producing *Busmen* in 1932, which depicted the coronation bus strikes (Chambers, 1989). Theatre Union, founded by theatre makers Joan Littlewood and Ewan MacColl (then Jimmie Miller), also took up the form in the late 1930s, affirming the significance of Living Newspapers to the agit-prop, leftist, and radical theatre practice of the UK in the mid twentieth century. In Brazil, inflections of the form can be read through Augusto Boal's *Teatro Jornal* (Newspaper Theatre), which emerged in 1971 from the practice of the Nucleus Group of the Teatro de Arena in São Paulo (Brazil) during the military dictatorship (1964–1985). As the news media itself, and the ways in which we encounter it, has continued to develop and expand so too have Living Newspapers. Digital iterations of the Living Newspaper have emerged since the turn of the twenty-first century. A leader in this practice UK-based company C&T has utilised digital practices to undertake international and networked Living Newspaper projects with people in the USA, Australia, and Japan.

Due to its location at the intersection with a range of performance forms and historical movements, scholarship surrounding the Living Newspaper has appeared in the intersecting areas of popular and people's theatre (Bradby and McCormick, 1978; Kruger, 1992), political theatre (Leach, 2005), and documentary theatre (Forsythe and Megson, 2009; Youker, 2017). Scholarly works that specifically explore Living Newspapers tend to undertake an in-depth analysis of a particular context or singular case study, in this Element we aim to bring different examples from a range of contexts into conversation with one another. We undertake a close analysis of examples from Brazil, Russia, South Africa, the USA, and the UK to trace the global and local practices of Living Newspapers. The examples covered in this Element also address the full span of history of the form, from the early twentieth century to the emergence of the COVID-19 pandemic at the start of the 2020s. We engage with the Royal Court's *A Counter Narrative* across each section of the Element for three reasons: 1) its emergence in a period of unprecedented global crisis offers a unique opportunity to reflect on how the Living Newspaper is shaped by and imbued with the qualities of crisis; 2) the Royal Court project marked the largest scale Living Newspaper produced by a single theatre company in the twenty-first century, a period that has seen significant shifts in how news is produced and consumed; 3) the expansiveness of *A Counter Narrative* is a productive holding frame for the central areas of analysis we are undertaking: employment, form, time, and space.

Locating Crisis and Crisis Theatre

While the performance strategies vary across context, Living Newspapers have consistently appeared during periods of crisis as a mode of enforcing or speaking back to power, a material intervention generating employment and a way to reimagine the cultural life of a nation. It is this persistence across crises that we are interested in exploring further. As Stuart Cosgrove notes, the Living Newspaper form is invariably bound up with political and social rupture: 'Perhaps more than any other cultural form, it thrives on the immediate demands of a major social crisis. The living newspaper is a drama of revolution, civil war and economic depression: a theatre of political flashpoints' (Cosgrove, 1982: iii). In this Element, we propose Living Newspapers as an exemplary form to illuminate crisis theatre, concurrently we posit that using a lens of crisis theatre will offer new understandings of the Living Newspaper.

Performance scholars have previously taken up crisis as a moment to evaluate the theatrical landscape (Delgado and Svich, 2002) and to consider the potential of performance to build communal solidarity (Wallace and Escoda et al., 2022). Further, the ways in which prison theatre and refugee arts and performance are increasingly backgrounded by crisis rhetoric has been examined by Ashley E. Lucas (2020) and Alison Jeffers (2011), respectively. Vicky Angelaki identifies crisis as endemic at the outset of the twenty-first century, with a particular focus on the 2008 global financial crisis and the multifaceted social crises it produced. Angelaki illuminates how performance during this period 'absorbed [crisis] events [. . .], affected by them to its thematic and formal core; it is now reflecting them back unto the society that produced them' (2017: 5). Here, we build on the work of Angelaki but what distinguishes crisis theatre from performances *of* crisis is that the production is in itself a material interventionist action that directly responds to the state of crisis. Crisis theatre emerges from *inside* the urgent phase of crisis, rather than in the period of recovery that follows it, and consequently it is enmeshed in this state of disruption that it is formulated by the characteristics of crisis beyond the content the performance itself.

The ways in which political and social crisis are infused into performance has also been explored by Diana Taylor in her work on Latin American plays, written between 1965 and 1970. For Taylor, a key feature of 'the theatre of crisis' is its capturing of both 'the objective systemic shifts or ruptures (revolution, military takeovers, wars and civil wars) that affect the nature of the society as a whole and the subjective, personal experience of disorientation and loss of identity' (Taylor, 1991). Our investigation of crisis theatre in these pages is also attentive to the ways in which the Living Newspaper brings objective and subjective encounters with crisis into contact with one another. The content of Living Newspapers tends to evoke the ways in which the political and the personal meet. Further in attending to Living Newspapers and their dramaturgy, we show how they contain and stage ruptures in individual and collective experiences of time and space through their production, structure, and dissemination. So, beyond Angelaki's 'absorption' of crisis in theme and form and Taylor's recognition of theatre as capturing the objective and subjective experience of emergency, crisis theatre assumes the specific conditions of crisis in its material practices, temporalities, and spatial logics

In developing a framework for what we are calling *crisis theatre*, our engagement with crisis is underpinned by crisis management scholarship. Emerging as a discrete field in the late twentieth century, crisis research expanded rapidly alongside the increasing interconnectedness and mediatisation that marked this period of globalisation. Given we argue that crisis theatre is performance born of crisis, it is productive to turn to crisis management scholarship as it illuminates how crises are handled as they unfold. In these pages we do not only address crisis itself but, through a focus on the Living Newspaper as crisis theatre, we are interested in how such performance navigates moments of rupture or states of emergency from inside the crisis. Holding crisis management alongside the Living Newspaper offers insights into how theatre aligns with and works through models of crisis management in periods of social, political, and economic turmoil.

In this Element we take up Arjen Boin, Uriel Rosenthal, and Louise K. Comfort's definition of crisis as: 'periods of upheaval and collective stress, disturbing everyday patterns and threatening core values and structures of a social system in unexpected, often unconceivable, ways' (2001: 6). Across this body of scholarship there is a recognition of crisis as a fundamental disruption, often communally experienced, that shifts the linear progression of the past into the future and reorients the ways in which we situate ourselves in our society. Writing in 2001, Boin, Rosenthal, and Comfort also assert the particular identity of modern crises, which are no longer 'a discrete event, but a process unfolding as manifold forces interact in unforeseen and disturbing ways. Modern crises are increasingly characterized by complexity, interdependence, and politicisation' (2001: 6). This networked experience of interlocking and multifaceted crises has been prevalent over the first two decades of the twenty-first century, with the global financial crisis; uprisings that stretch across territories such as the Arab Spring and Anti-Extradition Hong Kong protests; geopolitical wars in Afghanistan, Iraq, Syria, and Ukraine; the environmental emergency; and the global COVID-19 pandemic. Here, we are interested in exploring how crisis impacts the dramaturgies of the Living Newspaper.

Our conceptualisation of crises recognises them as inherently social and political processes. An event or situation is only deemed a crisis 'when people perceive something as an urgent threat [. . .]. A collective perception of threat may arise organically, or it might be constructed' (Boin, Ekengren, and Rhinard, 2020: 121). To define and assert something as a crisis produces particular actions and material responses that would not arise if the term crisis was not invoked. There are, of course, objective and empirical crises that inflict material damage such as natural disasters, cyber-attacks, or outbreaks of disease. However, even in these instances there is a social underpinning to the encounter with crisis: who has been put at risk and who has been protected in the preparation and responses for such disasters. So, as Rosenthal and Kouzmin assert, critically attending to 'crises provides a unique laboratory of social and political life' (1993: 8). Fundamentally, an examination of crisis illuminates where systems have been neglected or made resilient; who is exposed, and who is relied upon; what narratives emerge about value, power, and care.

In the following sections, we offer a set of logics through which we intend to identify and interrogate Living Newspapers: their material potential (Section 1), aesthetic imperatives (Section 2), spatial and digital practices (Section 3), and temporal dimensions (Section 4). We propose that this reveals a set of qualities that might be applied to a broader set of performance practices we would categorise as crisis theatre. Such theatre might produce a wider access to material and financial opportunities during periods of economic rupture. It can engage directly with the questions of around the value of culture during periods of turmoil. Crisis theatre utilises accessible, reproducible, disseminatable forms that can be scaled up or down depending on the available resources in a way that facilitates the engagement of a broad group of theatre makers and audiences and fosters the sharing of performance during periods of upheaval. Site and locatedness is fundamental to crisis theatre due to its intrinsic responsiveness to its context; concurrently such theatre is often networked in its practice, engaging with mediated communication in its content, and increasingly digitally realised. Finally, crisis theatre is responsive and foregrounds temporality in ways that support theatre makers and audiences to engage with their felt experiences of time during moments of rupture.

In Section 1 we take up an exploration of the Federal Theatre Project and *A Counter Narrative*, foregrounding exploring the material interventions of culture during economic turmoil. Then we examine *Born in the RSA*, Augusto Boal's *Teatro Jornal,* and the Royal Court project in Section 2 to understand how theatre operates as a form of collective worldmaking during periods of censorship, suppression, and disinformation. Section 3 considers the ways in which mediatisation is a fundamental quality of the Living Newspapers, reflecting on how this quality shapes its relation to space and digital spheres of production through an exploration of the Blue Blouses public performances in early twentieth century Russia, C&T's engagement of young people in digital spaces at the outset of the twenty-first century, and *A Counter Narrative*'s move across digital and physical modalities. Finally, Section 4 examines the specific temporalities of crisis at play in the Living Newspaper and in moments of crisis.

1 Global Crises and Material Interventions

Drawing on established histories of Living Newspapers as an arts-based employment intervention, this section attends to the arts emergency that accompanied the COVID-19 pandemic in the UK and considers it alongside the work of the Federal Theatre Project during the Great Depression in the USA, asking what it means to materially invest in theatre practice during periods of crisis. We trace the emergence of the Federal Theatre Project, and the controversies that surrounded it, reflecting on the ideological battle around culture in crisis that it held within it. Alongside this, we consider how the Royal Court's Living Newspaper project was distinctive in turning to this model of performance in the economic fallout of the COVID-19 pandemic for UK-based theatre workers, creating significant work and commissioning opportunities for artists, performers, and technical staff relative to a theatre of its size. We examine the make-up of the theatre makers engaged by both the Royal Court and the Federal Theatre Project, asserting the uneven impacts of crisis on individuals who are already marginalised or under-represented in the theatre industry (due to their race, gender, disability, or age) and reflecting on the ways in which these examples sought to intervene in some of these inequalities. We begin by examining state funding of the arts in two discrete period of crisis – the Great Depression of the 1930s and the COVID-19 pandemic of the 2020s – and in two distinct national contexts (USA and UK) with different underlying attitudes to the public funding of culture. In doing so, we illuminate the resonances in discourse and practice that emerge when culture receives state funding during a period of crisis.

Governmental Arts Provision in Times of Crisis: 1930s USA and the UK in 2020

The Federal Theatre Project operated between 1935 and 1939 and sat within the broader set of social and economic programmes that formed the New Deal in the USA in the 1930s. The introduction of New Deal policies was an attempt to ameliorate the effects of the depression that followed the global economic collapse between 1929 and 1933. In the USA this saw unemployment rise to 25 per cent, wages reduce by 42 per cent and productivity fall by two thirds (FDR Library, n.d.). Collectively, the New Deal policies were intended to encourage the USA's economic recovery in a period of global recession and consisted of a significant expansion of public infrastructure investment, increased financial regulation, and the introduction of welfare and public works programmes in order to reduce unemployment. The Works Progress Administration was established in 1935 to oversee the latter and employed over eight and a half million people in construction, public works, maintenance, education, and cultural roles during its eight-year history.

A central tenet of the Works Progress Administration was Federal Project No. 1, a historic and unparalleled investment in arts and culture in the USA, which sought 'to provide employment for qualified artists, musicians, actors, and authors' and ultimately consisted of the Federal Art, Music, Theatre, and Writers' Projects; and until October 1936, the Historical Records Survey. At their peak these projects employed vast numbers of creatives: 5,300 visual artists and related professionals were hired by the Federal Art Project; the Federal Music Project employed around 16,000 musicians; the Federal Writers Project engaged 6,686 writers; and the Federal Theatre Project employed 12,700 theatre workers (Adams and Goldbard, 1985: n.p). As well as developing and sharing new works, these creatives were also involved in significantly expanding the provision of creative arts education across the USA and supported the cataloguing and archiving of existing music and visual arts materials to ensure work was documented in public institutions.

Within this context, the Works Progress Administration hired Hallie Flanagan, an established playwright, director, and producer, to lead the Federal Theatre Project. In 'Instructions: Federal Theatre Projects', a document outlining the organisation and aims of the project for theatre workers around the country, Flanagan asserts:

> The primary aim of the Federal Theatre Project, is the reemployment of theatre workers now on public relief rolls: actors, directors, playwrights, designers, vaudeville artists, stage technicians, and other workers in the theatre field.
>
> The far-reaching purpose is the establishment of theatres so vital to community life that they will continue to function after the program of this Federal Project is completed. (1935)

The overarching focus of the project was thus two-fold: to respond to the immediate economic crisis that had left theatre workers destitute; and to harness this previously unmatched investment in a programme of theatre making that was intended to reach the length and breadth of the USA, in order to try and weave publicly funded theatre into the cultural life of the nation. The Federal Theatre Project cost an estimated 46 million dollars, attracting 65,000,000 people to theatrical events and employing over 12,000 artists (Ross, 1974). As visual artist employed by the WPA, Harold Lehman asserted 'artists, formerly ignored by government, achieved a place in society they never could have reached otherwise – due to active government support for the arts' (Lehman in Opdycke, 2016). Exploring Living Newspapers as an employment intervention in the context of 1930s USA then illuminates the material impact of such projects but also underscores the ideological argument that artists and culture have a public value beyond crisis.

By investing in the arts, as well as communal infrastructure, during this period of crisis Franklin D. Roosevelt's government asserted an intrinsic value of public access to culture. However, the implementation of the Federal Theatre Project was not without resistance, indeed as Barry B. Witham notes the introduction of a federally subsidised theatre to generate labour for theatre workers on relief roles was challenged from all sides:

> For the Broadway crowd they were amateurs. For the unions they were scabbers and a threat to their closed shops. For many of their WPA colleagues they were lazy bums. And for many politicians – at both a federal and local level – they were a visible threat to America, especially American capitalism. (Witham, 2003: 5)

Creatives who were able to access the limited employment opportunities that remained felt the introduction of the Federal Theatre Project would lead to a debasing of theatre by virtue of it being produced by those not able to gain professional work. Similarly, the unions were distrustful of the introduction of the Federal Theatre Project due to the relief wages of $23.86 per week that the state paid as standard and the potential for this to undermine hard fought wage and labour rights in the theatre industry. Additionally, there was some public resistance in relation to the value culture brought to the economy, comparative to investment in infrastructure or public buildings. Finally, a number of politicians articulated such an endeavour as a threat to the national culture and the capitalist economic system that the theatre industry stood as a shining example of.

As concerns about a state-funded intervention emerged from various stakeholders in the arts, the Federal Theatre Project's relationship with its funder (the US Congress) was also often fraught. Arthur Arent's *Ethiopia,* intended to be the first Living Newspaper staged as part of the Federal Theatre Project, depicted the invasion of the East African nation by Italian dictator Benito Mussolini and the exile of, Emperor of Ethiopia, Haile Selassie. However, the production was cancelled at the last minute due to what the State Department deemed incendiary representations of foreign heads of state. This anxiety subsequently led to a government directive preventing any Federal Theatre Project production from depicting foreign ministers. Ultimately the show never ran, instead the company held a single open rehearsal for friends and reporters to attend. The ill-fated first Living Newspaper illuminates the uneasy relationship between state-funded culture in the USA, particularly during a period of political crisis, and the material it produced.

Throughout its four-year existence the Federal Theatre Project endured a range of political controversies predominantly rooted in an unease about the content of productions; the Living Newspaper strand of the project produced work that was regularly critical of the government or the status quo in the country. *Triple-A Plowed Under* (1936) criticised the Agricultural Adjustment Act of 1933 and its impact on farmers; *Injunction Granted* (1937) traced a history of working class struggle for labour rights in the USA against employers and state institutions, asserting that solidarity and fighting for a common cause was the only way to effect change; *One Third of a Nation* (1938) illuminated the housing crisis and rise of slums in the USA, pointing to the inadequacy of the legislative response from the government. Alongside staging explicit critiques of the government, the state-funded cultural project sought to promote class consciousness in its productions; working with theatre makers across racial boundaries in the segregated USA; and prioritised access to state-funded culture in parts of the country which had previously had none. That the US government would fund culture to this degree was a radical departure; that it facilitated such critical work – in themes and practices – provoked a fierce debate around investments in culture and what how such work was intertwined with visions of the nation itself.

This perception of the Federal Theatre Project as antagonistic to the state eventually resulted in its closure following a review by The House Committee on Un-American Activities, which cast the project as led by communists or communist sympathisers: 'It is apparent from the startling evidence received thus far that the Federal Theatre Project not only is serving as a branch of the Communistic organization but is also one more link in the vast and unparalleled New Deal propaganda machine' (J. Parnell Thomas in Raymond, 1945). There were also racist overtones to the committee's investigation as the Federal Theatre Project's Negro Theatre Unit was a recurrent focus in the hearings (despite its relatively small size), with committee members criticising the promotion of Black culture through this strand of the project and asserting the project as an enabler in interracial dating. Flanagan offered a spirited defence of the Federal Theatre Project under questioning,

> It is the widest and most American base that any theater has ever built upon, and I request you not only to write that into the record but to read the list of public schools and universities and churches and the civic and social groups that are supporting this Federal Theater. (Flanagan in US Congress, 1938: 2867)

In asserting the project as historic movement towards a theatre for the people in the USA, Flanagan sought to appeal to the democratic ideals that supposedly underpinned the committee's mission. Indeed, the project *was* and continues to be an enviable case study in civic engagement through cultural practice with its national reach, integration of professional and non-professional performers, collaboration across artforms and geographical boundaries. However, following the hearings, the US Congress defunded the project in June of 1939.

To mark the termination of the Federal Theatre Project, The Children's Theatre Unit adapted their production of *Pinocchio* in New York. On closing night, the show ended with the staging of a funeral for Pinocchio, who stood in for the Federal Theatre Project, and an improvised procession was taken out into the streets. As Flanagan recounts,

> Pinocchio, having conquered selfishness and greed, did not become a living boy. Instead he was turned back into a puppet. 'So let the bells proclaim our grief', intone the company at the finish, 'that his small life was all too brief'. The stagehands knocked down the sets in full view of the audience and the company laid Pinocchio away in a pine box which bore the legend: BORN DECEMBER 23, 1938; KILLED BY AN ACT OF CONGRESS, JUNE 30, 1939. (Flanagan, 1969: 364–5)

The introduction of Federal Arts One in a period of crisis was perceived by some as a threat to the ideological underpinnings of capitalism and lauded by others as a potential mechanism to restructure the ways in which culture was made and accessed in the USA. Beyond these binary positions, the turn to culture during a period of crisis offered a momentary space to imagine a reformed landscape of arts practice in the USA, one that significantly broadened access to culture and cultural work and one that was supported by the state.

In 2020, COVID-19 brought debates around the value of culture into sharp focus. As cultural economists Mark Banks and Justin O'Connor assert, in their writing on responses to the arts emergency that accompanied the pandemic,

> what this crisis is illuminating, in all-too-lurid detail, is how we think about and value art and culture; how we argue for their importance; how governments and public policy actors understand and value them, what they are prepared to do, on what grounds and with what capacity. (Banks & O'Connor, 2021: 3)

To examine state responses and resourcing of culture in moments of political, social, and economic rupture foregrounds an analysis of how public value is quantified in relation to arts and culture. Crises, particularly the economic collapse of the 1930s and the social and financial turmoil of the COVID-19 pandemic, invoke a narrative of scarcity (real or fabricated) from governments and those in positions of power. To invest resource into culture during such a period holds the potential to imbue culture with a transformative status, as the Federal Theatre Project demonstrates. However, investment in culture during the COVID-19 pandemic highlights the complexity of decisions around who gets to attribute value, and to what, during a crisis.

The COVID-19 pandemic required immediate health responses, causing unparalleled disruption to global financial markets and demanding significant communal action from publics while understandings of the virus were still developing. Labour markets across the world were severely impacted. In the UK the number of people in work fell by 825,000 from March 2020 to December 2020; redundancies reached record highs; and the number of people claiming unemployment benefits doubled between March and May 2020 (Francis-Devine, Powell, and Clark, 2022). Across the UK cultural sector arts organisations closed their doors, freelancers lost work, and full time staff were made redundant. The Office for National Statistics reported that the arts and entertainment industry saw a 44.5 per cent reduction in monthly gross domestic product (GDP) output in the three months up to June 2020 compared with the three months earlier. On 20 March 2020 the UK Government introduced the Coronavirus Job Retention Scheme (CJRS), which provided grants to employers to furlough workers with the government funding 80 per cent of employees' wages (up to £2500 per month), in addition to employer pension and National Insurance contributions. The CJRS was intended to prevent mass unemployment and ensure workers would continue to be paid despite the impact of the pandemic on the finances and operation of businesses. Approximately 70 per cent of workers in the arts and entertainment sector were furloughed under the government scheme, the second highest after accommodation and food services (Tobin, 2020). These figures demonstrate the significant impact the coronavirus had on the arts industry, marking it as one of the sectors worst hit by the pandemic.

For theatres, a mandate against collective gathering struck the core of theatre making and the performance event. A Department for Culture, Media and Sport report outlined in July 2020,

> The COVID 19 crisis presents the biggest threat to the UK's cultural infrastructure, institutions and workforce in a generation. The loss of performing arts institutions, and the vital work they do in communities by spreading the health and education benefits of cultural engagement, would undermine the aims of the Government's 'levelling up' agenda and Arts Council England's next 10-year strategy, and reverse decades of progress in cultural provision and diversity and inclusion that we cannot afford to lose. (Digital, Culture, Media and Sport Committee, 2020)

As the pandemic continued to unfold, it became increasingly evident that the significant economic and health crisis presented an existential threat to both the creative workforce and cultural infrastructure. The government had made available a £160 million Emergency Response Fund distributed by the Arts Council England, broken down into: £90 million for National Portfolio Organisations (i.e. companies in receipt of regular ACE funding); £50 million for organisations outside of the regular funding portfolio; and £20 million for individual practitioners. While this seems a significant investment, the arts and culture sector in the UK has an annual turnover of £17 billion. With all venues closed indefinitely and the substantial loss of work opportunities, the Emergency Response Fund was less than 1 per cent of the sector's yearly turnover.

Across the UK theatre makers, unions, venues, and politicians were calling for targeted support. In April 2020, 100 leading creatives who wrote an open letter to Boris Johnson (then Prime Minister), Rishi Sunak (then Chancellor), and Oliver Dowden (then Cultural Secretary), underscoring the scale of the crisis and stating half of creative organisations in the UK, thought that their financial reserves would not last beyond June 2020 (Norbury, 2020). Broadcasting Entertainment Communications and Theatre Union (BECTU); the Society of London Theatres; and the Creative Industries Federation made repeated calls for government support, appealing to the relative size of the workforce, rapid growth of the arts and cultural industries within the UK economy, and fragility of cultural ecosystems as rationales for targeted support for the sector. While governments in France, Germany, and New Zealand, all announced significant targeted support for their cultural sectors, the UK continued to point organisations towards existing general support: the self-employment income support scheme, the job retention scheme, business rates holidays.

Following five months of campaigning and advocacy from workers in the cultural sector, the UK Government eventually announced The Cultural Recovery Fund (CRF), a £1.57 billion rescue package for the UK's arts, culture, and heritage industries on 5 July 2020. The measures included: £1.15 billion of funding for cultural organisations in England, comprised of £270 million of loans and £880 million in grants; £100 million of targeted support for organisations deemed national cultural institutions in England; £120 million capital investment to restart construction on cultural infrastructure that was derailed due to the pandemic. The package also included an extra £188 million for the devolved administrations in Northern Ireland (£33 million), Scotland (£97 million), and Wales (£59 million) (Tobin, 2020). As with Federal Arts One, the CRF grants were monumental in terms of investment in the arts, marking the largest *direct* distribution of state funding to the arts in the UK since the establishment of the arm's length Arts Council of Great Britain in 1946. This support was hard fought for and marked a substantial recovery package for the sector, which would pull it back from the brink of collapse. As with the Federal Theatre Project, however, the politics of who received funding remained complex, further illuminating the notion of the *kinds* of culture that is deemed valuable, and asserting the ways in which this value is amplified in periods of crisis.

Organisations needed to demonstrate they were 'culturally significant' to access support from the CRF. Indeed, when announcing the package, Culture Secretary Oliver Dowden stated his desire to 'prioritise those institutions that need it most, starting with the crown jewels of our national life – Royal Albert Halls and so on' (Dowden, 2020). Dowden's comment was met with concern by creative leaders who affirmed the importance of all parts of the cultural ecosystem. In the first round of grants and loans more than £165 million in repayable finance was offered to England's famous cultural organisations, including the National Theatre, Southbank Centre, the Royal Albert Hall and the Royal Shakespeare Company, Royal Opera House, English National Opera, and Historic Palaces. In these targeted loans then, there is an implicit desire to sustain the cultural bemouths that perform a specific national cultural identity. This funding round also saw London-based organisations receive nearly a third of all the money allocated. In subsequent evaluations of the fund, the government have acknowledged the London-centric nature of the allocation, but argued that

> parts of the country had less 'cultural and heritage fabric' than others. It asserted that the fund aimed to support existing organisations at risk of failure, rather than to create new cultural infrastructure where it did not currently exist. (Committee of Public Accounts, 2021: 12)

This is directly opposed to the vision of culture that was heralded by Federal Arts One in the 1930s, which sought to utilise the moment of crisis and the unprecedented state investment in culture that accompanied it, to expand the provision of arts programmes and cultural events to areas and populations that previously had limited or no access to it. The ideology underpinning the UK government's funding of culture during the COVID-19 pandemic was one of maintaining the status quo rather than taking the opportunity to reimagine what public culture might look like. There was a focus on maintaining the existing cultural eco-system and structures that distribute resources, with most funds going to arts organisations or cultural building rather than directly to freelancers. This is particularly significant given that freelancers make up 49 per cent of the creative workforce in the cultural sector (Henley, 2022). The Cultural Recovery Fund, therefore sought to maintain existing systems of redistribution and gatekeeping that existed within the arts landscape. In the case of COVID-19 and state funding in the UK, the debate is not around the public value of culture but rather around the delineation of which kinds of culture created by and for whom is deemed valuable and most in need of saving.

The Living Newspaper as Employment Intervention

The Living Newspaper Unit was a specific programme within the Federal Theatre Project. While there have been conflicting accounts of who initiated the turn to the Living Newspaper form as a part of the broader project, histories most consistently assert that this decision emerged out of a series of conversations between Flanagan, playwright Elmer Rice, and Morris Watson who was Head of The Newspaper Guild. Underpinning the choice of form was the sheer scale of the project, with its initial aim to employ 10,000 unemployed creatives, and a desire to broaden the scope to support the unemployed newspaper workers. As Flanagan recounts, Rice could not fathom how such a theatre project might generate enough work for all the creatives they sought to move off relief roles, 'Elmer Rice Kept saying. "Even with twenty plays in rehearsal at once, with thirty in a cast, that would keep only a fraction of them busy"' (Flannagan in Quinn, 2021). Keen to find a solution to vast scale, Flannagan suggested, 'We wouldn't use them all in plays – we could do living newspapers. We could dramatize the news with living actors, light, music, movement' (Flannagan in Quinn, 2021). Concurrently Rice was meeting with Watson who he recounts, 'asked me if I couldn't do something for unemployed newspaper men. At first, I couldn't see how they would fit into a theatre project. But as we talked it over, the idea of doing a sort of animated newsreel evolved' (Rice in Arent, 1968: 16).

The particular form of the Living Newspaper requires a significant and ongoing body of workers to execute: researchers and writers to investigate, capture, and edit the ongoing news cycle; artists and designers to produce a series of shifting and varied worlds out of scenography, props, costumes; and directors and performers to bring new work relevant to different audiences across the country. The combination of the collaboration with the Newspaper Guild and the sheer scale of the project's ambition meant that the Living Newspapers it produced remain central to the ways the Federal Theatre Project intervened in the political, cultural, and economic landscape of the 1930s and are core to the later historicisation of the project.

While in 2020 the Royal Court were not working in collaboration with journalists, the impetus to find a form that offered the capacity to provide a wide range of employment for a relatively significant number of creatives was much the same. In evidence submitted in June 2020 to a UK parliamentary committee on the Impact of COVID-19 in the cultural sector the theatre's Executive Producer, Lucy Davies, stated that the pandemic instigated the:

> Immediate closure of the theatre for an indefinite period with suspension of 8 productions and a UK tour [. . .]. Four income streams choked off [ticket, touring, catering, fundraising]. This amounts to a loss of around £2 m over the 5-month lockdown. (Davies, 2020)

The theatre furloughed around 100 workers, with 18 permanent staff continuing to work in post. Davies, however, noted that each year the theatre work with around 370 freelancers, noting despite honouring or deferring all contracts '[t] hese people are losing work with us' (Davies, 2020). In this same submitted evidence Davies questions:

> conceptually, theatre will survive this rupture [. . .]. So what is the ethical approach to a 12–18 month rupture? [. . .] Do we need to re-imagine an art form that is defined by public gathering and physical space into a digital one, and what risks come with that? (Davies, 2020)

The fundamental idea of theatre as a collective and communal practice would endure, but the challenge was around how to respond rapidly to the material impact of the pandemic in such a way that the specialist workers would endure as well and return to the industry following this rupture.

Following awards from Arts Council England's Emergency Response Fund and Cultural Recovery Funding in July and August 2020, respectively, the Royal Court sought to address this question with the announcement that they would reopen with *Living Newspaper: A Counter Narrative.* Artistic Director Vicky Featherstone stated the objectives of the project were:

> quite simple, to give as many people as possible work, to bring our theatre back to life and to create something which is urgent, dynamic, political and disruptive – acknowledging the hugely changed and changing times. (Royal Court, 2020)

This echoes Flanagan's first articulation of the Federal Theatre Project and indeed Featherstone explicitly asserts this as a central inspiration for the Court, noting this programme also sought 'to mobilise and employ unemployed artists and theatre workers' in the wake of the Great Depression in 1930s USA.[1] By the close of Edition Seven in May 2021, the Royal Court had employed over 300 freelance creatives, in six months nearly matching the number of freelancers they typically employ in a year. The scale of the material intervention the Court delivered in the form of employment provision was therefore a significant and swift response to the crisis theatre workers faced in the initial stages of the pandemic. As outlined above, the *form* of the Living Newspaper is able to generate significant workloads for theatre workers due to the model of artistic production it demands, one that is continuously producing new work, which is responsive to a shifting news cycle and therefore requires a making and remaking of new worlds for audiences to encounter.

The turn to this form in a time of crisis is a chance to open up creative employment, but open it up to who? Flanagan was assured that the Federal Theatre Project opened the possibility for an inclusive people's theatre in the USA, one that represented Americans across racial, class, and geographical boundaries. However, Rena Fraden has traced the internal conflicts that dogged Flanagan's liberal ideal of the Federal Theatre, namely that it was both professional and open to all; predicated on the value of an experimental theatre but local companies regularly wanted to stage work from the American canon; in receipt of state funding but with a desire to create agitational theatre, which was occasionally censored by the state (Fraden, 1996). Fraden specifically examines the conflicts surrounding the establishment of sixteen Negro Theatre Units, which operated in twenty-three cities across the USA and specifically focused on creating employment opportunities for Black writers, performers, musicians and producing performance that engaged Black communities (Ross, 1974).[2] In the development

[1] The theatre actually invited journalist and academic Stuart Cosgrove to write an article on the history of the Federal Theatre Project to contextualise the Royal Court's project. It is available here: https://royalcourttheatre.com/the-origins-of-the-living-newspaper/

[2] Negro Theatre Units were established in Hartford, Boston, Salem, Newark, and Philadelphia, Raleigh, Atlanta, Birmingham, and New Orleans, Cleveland, Detroit, Peoria, and Chicago, and Seattle, Portland, Los Angeles and New York.

of Federal Theatre Project, Flanagan had collaborated with leading Black and African American artists, primarily actress Rose McClendon, who suggested the need for separate companies in order to ensure investment in plays that addressed themes relevant to the Black and African American citizens and supported the provision of theatrical employment for these communities. The Negro Theatre Units illuminate the ambition of the Federal Theatre Project, during segregation, to invest in a model of culture that represents a range of American experience. However, as Fraden notes, the creation of the units was replete with contradiction. The appointment of directors for these units, and whether they should be headed by Black artists, was contested both by the leaders of the Federal Theatre Project and by the Black and African American creatives who made up the membership of the Units (ibid). Ultimately, in a 'compromise palatable to all factions' the Harlem units were led by a collaboration between McClendon and white director John Houseman, with a view to the unit moving to being entirely Black led over time.[3]

Beyond the politics around the membership and leadership of the Negro Theatre Units, there was a notable absence of Living Newspapers produced by Black playwrights. Theatre historian Paul Nadler traces the histories of three unproduced Living Newspapers (Elmer Rice's *The South*; Ward Courtney's *Stars and Bars*; and Abram Hill and John Silvera's *Liberty Defferred*) to illuminate the ways in which Living Newspapers addressing racial oppression were either embroiled in bureaucracy and in-fighting at the Federal Theatre Project or deemed too challenging to stage as part of a state-funded project with national reach. Nadler concludes:

> these plays may have suffered from the very power of their genre. The living-newspaper form drops the shield of fiction, confronting issues not as imaginative or Platonic concepts, but as questions of immediate concern to a living, breathing audience. The Federal Theatre dared to drop the shield to present agriculture, housing, labor relations, public health, and other controversial subjects on stage. But race was and is among the most visceral, emotional, and divisive issues in America. (Nadler, 1995: 621)

Despite the emphasis on the vitality of Living Newspapers' form as part of the Federal Theatre Project, the project failed to produce a Living Newspaper that was thematically focused on race in the USA. There were some successes in the Federal Theatre Project's attempts at diversifying the cultural workforce of the USA; during this period the Federal Theatre Project became the largest employer of Black people

[3] Although John Houseman and Orson Welles are frequently credited as the initial co-directors of the Harlem Unit, Jay Plum has traced Rose McClendon's distinct contributions to the Federal Theatre Project in 'Rose McClendon and the Black Units of the Federal Theatre Project: A Lost Contribution' (*Theatre Survey*, 33, 1992).

in Harlem during The Great Depression. However, the efficacy of the project was made complicated by its tentative approach to deploying a theatrical form anchored in critique to stage Black and African American creatives experiences.

Following the 'return to normal' researchers have sought to document the impact and consequences that COVID-19 has had on the cultural sector, particularly in relation to freelance creatives. A clear trend has emerged illuminating that the pandemic served to intensify existing inequalities, as with many other areas of society, in the arts and cultural sector (Walmsley et al., 2022). Researchers at The Centre for Cultural Value found that '[t]hose individuals and communities who were already under-represented in the cultural workforce were more likely to leave cultural jobs in 2020 than those who already dominated many key roles in the cultural sector and wider economy' (Walmsley et al., 2022: 4). Beyond further entrenching pre-existing inequalities relating to race, caring responsibilities, disability, and class for example, the pandemic has also resulted in a loss of labour (Walmsley et al., 2022: 56). Prior to the pandemic freelancers 'constituted 62% of the core creative workforce [. . .] and only 52% at the end of 2020' (Walmsley et al., 2022: 65). In music, performing and visual arts specifically the number of workers in these areas 'dropped from around 200,000 in January-March to around 160,000 in April-June and then again to around 145,000 in July-September, a decline of almost 30% since pre-lockdown' (Owen, O'Brien, and Taylor, 2020). As outlined above, against a background of sweeping job losses the Royal Court employed almost the equivalent number of freelance creatives, across the six month production of *A Counter Narrative*, as in a standard producing year. While an unparalleled intervention in the UK theatre sector, it is challenging to determine how the project sits in relation to the existing inequalities of the theatre sector. At the time of writing, the Royal Court has not released data relating to the race, ethnicity, class, gender, sexuality, disability, or age of those employed across the project or how this compares to their hiring practices in a typical year. However, Associate Director at the Royal Court Lucy Morrison has outlined the ways in which the theatre was particularly attentive to early career creatives during the production of their Living Newspapers. Indeed, the Office for National Statistics has found that age became a determining marker of freelancers' experiences during the pandemic: 'the crisis for freelancers is hitting different demographic groups in uneven ways. Age clearly matters, with the decline in numbers of freelance workers impacting less severely on the oldest, and perhaps most established, freelancers' (Florisson et al., 2021).

Inspired by the online mentorship of a group of six early career designers by the Royal Court's Resident Designer, following concern about how the pandemic would impact the next generation of designers coming through,

A Counter Narrative carved space for early career creatives across the project. The aforementioned mentees worked on the Living Newspaper design, a commitment was made for each edition to have a distinct acting company with at least two recent graduates, to maximise employment opportunities. The theatre wrote to over 100 writers, from early career and emerging to mid-career and established, inviting them to contribute to the shaping and evolution of the Living Newspaper structure developed and deployed by the Royal Court. For the acting company there was a commitment to it being a new company for each edition to maximise the opportunity for as many actors as possible through the project and that each company would have at least two recent graduates. In addition to these priorities that were threaded through *A Counter Narrative*, Edition Seven was written by a group of writers aged fourteen to twenty-one. As the copy for this edition announced: ‘This is the time to listen to writers who haven’t been heard before’ (Royal Court Theatre, 2021a). This statement asserting the utility of this moment of rupture to encounter the work of young and early career artists. While the project was rooted in the histories and lineages of Living Newspapers, in the prioritising of opportunities for emerging theatre makers there was very much a focus on the future of the industry.

Conclusion

By holding together the Federal Theatre Project and the Royal Court’s response to the pandemic we highlight the ways in which a turn to culture during crisis is a recurrent impulse and a persistent battleground. Throughout this Element we will examine other examples of Living Newspapers, which emerge out of this same battleground. Here, we have identified the Living Newspaper as a form that can engage a large workforce and consequently generate significant employment opportunities. This marks it as particularly suited to responding to economic or labour market turmoil and demonstrates the distinct potential and material interventions this form might offer in such moments. Crisis, in this instance, is an opportunity to break from business as usual and can therefore be an opportunity to reimagine what culture might look like, how it might be funded, who might engage with it, and who might create it.

2 The World in Pictures: Newspaper Aesthetics and Collective Worldmaking

The Living Newspaper has historically had a number of fundamental characteristics: an attention to contemporary events; use of multiple intersecting narratives and perspectives, themes and stylistic approaches; and a critical interrogation of 'the news' and its producers. However, theatre makers whose creative process is rooted in an engagement with the news have continued to experiment within the form. This has led to a proliferation of practices that fall within the parameters of Living Newspapers or push up against its boundaries. This section explores how by invoking the newspaper as a subject and strategy, Living Newspapers have constructed several aesthetic and formal approaches for performance to engage with, and intervene in, the world around us. Significantly, the relationship of the form to news media underscores its potential as a practice of worldmaking. The combination of news and performance offers a unique context in which to reflect on the ways in which both news media and theatre construct worlds in relation to our social and political realities. Throughout this section we will examine how three different examples – The Market Theatre's *Born in the RSA* (1985), Augusto Boal's Teatro Jornal (1971–), and the Royal Court's *A Counter Narrative* (2020–2021) – offer a distinct set of aesthetic frameworks, which we term 'newspaper aesthetics'.

We explore how newspaper aesthetics intersect with multiple forms (including documentary theatre, participatory performance, and new writing), to invite audiences to actively critique the content and positionality of the news. Further we reflect on how performances engaging with the news interrogate different modes of written media (the cartoon, the front page, the dating page, the obituary), asking questions around the hierarchies of writing at play within the newspaper and so illuminating the narratives, perspectives and voices that are given value. Living Newspapers offer an opportunity to remake the world we encounter through the news and also provide a platform to interrogate the aesthetics, politics, and ideologies that underpin the ways in which the news is constructed. Our exploration of newspaper aesthetics underscores the focus of these works on engendering critique, which as George Edmondson and Klaus Mladek underscore, shares the same etymology as crisis (from the Greek word κρίσις, or krísis). Edmondson and Mladek trace the historical separation of crisis as critique and crisis as a tumultuous occurrence in need of management, with the latter becoming increasingly removed from conceptualisations of crisis in the eighteenth century. Edmondson and Mladek argue for the reinsertion of critique to engagements with crisis: 'once we divest crisis of its etymological roots—once we drain krísis from crisis—we simultaneously deprive ourselves of the resolution and overcoming associated with crisis' (2017: 49). We assert that newspaper aesthetics are indicative of the ways in which this body of performance work seeks to reaffirm critique as central to crisis and key to overcoming it.

Worldmaking and the News

Newspapers are themselves world making mediums, reshaping and renegotiating understandings of how our lived experiences are constructed and situated in local, national, or global narratives. News partially produces our experience of the world, therefore in engaging with the news as content, aesthetic framework, and participatory practice Living Newspapers are uniquely positioned in relation to worldmaking. As sociologists William A. Gamson, David Croteau, William Hoynes, and Theodore Sasson have argued,

> We walk around with media-generated images of the world, using them to construct meaning about political and social issues. The lens through which we receive these images is not neutral but evidences the power and point of view of the political and economic elites who operate and focus it. And the special genius of this system is to make the whole process seem so normal and natural that the very art of social construction is invisible. (Gamson et al., 1992: 374)

Contemporary journalism occupies a blurred space between the communication of the realities of our world and the recognition of news media as a political actor that can challenge or reinforce entrenched systems of power. As media academic Catherine Adams' survey of the state of contemporary journalism scholarship identifies, there are overlapping and multiple shared understandings of journalism: a recognition that journalism should be rooted, factual, neutral, and proportional; the role of journalists as the Fourth Estate in 'holding the establishment to account', serving the public interest in illuminating new and relevant knowledge; and the significance of not just reporting but offering a critical and analytic engagement with the events and contexts explored (Adams, 2021). As Adams notes, when we examine the news, 'At stake is the public's understanding of current affairs, their historical context and the collective political memory, to enable informed decisions to be made. Journalism helps us to know the biases of history and understand the world' (Adams, 2021: 1165). Journalism helps publics collectively make meaning of our location in our histories and our interconnected present. The construction of the world through our engagement with the news is therefore deeply political and rooted in existing economies of power. Newspaper aesthetics become particularly significant in contexts where the news media itself is thrown into crisis; whether through censorship, oppressive regimes, or a destabilisation of media legitimacy in the twenty-first century. The examples of Living Newspapers addressed in this section consider the form against different contexts of crisis that orbit news media in apartheid South Africa, Brazil's military dictatorship, and the contested media landscape of the contemporary UK.

In taking up worldmaking as a frame through which to examine newspaper aesthetics, we attend to: 1) the socially and politically constructive nature of the news; and 2) the ongoing labour of making and remaking that is present in theatre that engages with how our lived realities are narrativised and communicated in the news. We particularly draw on Dorinne Kondo's articulation of the worldmaking potential of creative labour and theatrical representation, which she investigates as a race-making practice. Kondo's conceptualisation of worldmaking in performance emphasises its groundedness in social realities:

> we make, unmake, remake race within specific cultural and historical political economies. Making can be quotidian; it does not automatically conjure the divine sublime. 'Worldmaking' evokes sociopolitical transformation and the impossibility of escaping power, history, and culture. Worlds, like language, are pregiven, and remaking must always work with this givenness. (2018)

Kondo's acknowledgement of the contextual economies in which culture might seek to remake worlds is particularly useful in relation to newspaper aesthetics, which are acutely rooted in a social reality while also offering the opportunity to critically make and unmake how such realities are expressed to a broader public. Kondo's emphasis on worldmaking as a practice that works with the pregiven, is particularly relevant here. Newspaper aesthetics draw specifically on the 'pregiven' and stage both the existing sociopolitical landscape and, in some cases, its remaking. Beyond 'givenness', Kondo foregrounds the reparative process of worldmaking, which holds the potential to challenge existing social structures. That is, she proposes artistic production as 'reparative creativity', which holds a critical potential to offer 'articulations of redressive outrage' (2018: 33). Here we argue that worldmaking within newspaper aesthetics, when not used in service of state propaganda, can function as a mode of reparative creativity.

Performing the Real in a Period of Censorship

Living Newspapers have always been committed to politically inflected representations of the real through a collage of different performance strategies. In different contexts and periods of crisis, performances of 'the real' and narratives in the news become more contested. In this section, we consider the relationship between news, crisis, and performances of the real through an exploration of *Born in the RSA* (1985), produced at The Market Theatre in Johannesburg, considering the potential of the Living Newspaper form in a context of censorship and disinformation. Media censorship was a vital tool of the National Party government in South Africa throughout apartheid (1948–1994). As journalist (and, post-apartheid, prominent politician) Frene Ginwala noted in 1973, much of the press censorship that occurred was in part self-imposed by journalists and editors trying to navigate the complex and ambiguous legislation that surrounded publishing (Ginwala, 1973). For example, the Newspaper Press Union agreed to regulate its membership through its own Code of Conduct, introducing a clause stating: 'While the press retains its traditional right of criticism, comment should take cognisance of the complex racial problems in South Africa, the general good and the safety of the country and its people' (cited in Ginwala, 1973: 36). This was broadly perceived as an explicit agreement to not critique the apartheid regime and its constituent oppressions. In terms of legislation that explicitly underpinned the control of media narratives, the most significant was the Suppression of Communism Act 1950. This Act had wide reaching powers that enabled the government to close down newspapers and incarcerate journalists, or ban them from the premises of media outlets, if they were deemed to express views or disseminate information supporting the objectives of communism. In the apartheid context, this was used to persecute journalists and close down publications that supported the national liberation movement. More broadly, there was a multitude of legislation that journalists and editors needed to navigate, including: The Public Safety Act, which banned newspapers deemed to be publishing 'irresponsible' information; and The Entertainments (Censorship Act), which established The Publication and Entertainment Control Board, a body of censors to review drama, films, advertising, books, and other printed matter. Additionally, legislation related to specific state apparatus (e.g. police, prisons, education) limited what could be publicly reported about these areas. As Ginwala recounts, 'A South African editor once described the task of editing a paper in the country as "walking blindfolded through a minefield"'(Ginwala, 1973: 27). The legislative environment, coupled with a white supremacist government that institutionalised racial segregation, meant that newspapers were consistently negotiating layered and nuanced forms of censorship and state propaganda.

Theatre during this period was impacted by the state enforced segregation of spaces, people, and resources within the entertainment sectors. White and Afrikaans Theatres that prioritised non-political and imported commercial works were funded and promoted by the state. However, a diverse ecology of protest theatre flourished with the emergence of theatre organisations affiliated with the Black Consciousness Movement (e.g. South African Black Theatre Union and Theatre Council of Natal (TECON), and the Serpent Players); and other anti-apartheid resistance theatres that existed outside of state funding structures (e.g. The Market Theatre and Space Theatre). While in some ways theatre encountered less stringent controls than other media, numerous productions were closed or modified after being reviewed by Publication and Entertainment Control Board, with playwrights and companies detained due to the content of the work they created. Yet the theatre of resistance persisted and remained a significant forum in which South Africans sought to document the violence of the presiding regime and collectively imagine a different future. What then of theatrical forms that explicitly utilise news as a foundational characteristic of its process and aesthetic in this context of repression of the media and live performance?

Born in the RSA explores the lives of seven characters under apartheid and was devised by the cast (Vanessa Cooke, Timmy Kwebulana, Neil McCarthy, Gcina Mhlophe, Terry Norton, Thoko Ntshinga, and Fiona Ramsay) in collaboration with Barney Simon, playwright and co-founder of The Market Theatre. As the title alludes, all of the characters are born in the same place and yet, due to their race, their experience of the nation is disparate. Labour activist Thenjiwe, her sister art teacher sister Sindiswa, and their musician friend Zacharia are Black; anti-apartheid activist Susan, Mia a lawyer, housewife Nicky and her self-proclaimed politically neutral husband Glen are white. The central plot is underpinned by Glen becoming a police informer, which instigates the incarceration and torture of Thenjiwe and Susan. Parallel to this Thenjiwe's ten-year-old nephew, Dumisani, is wrongly arrested for his alleged participation in an children's protest, Sindiswa and Zacharia search for the ten year old, with the latter becoming increasingly incensed by the violent treatment of this young Black child. The play depicts the inescapability of becoming embroiled in the institutionally racist state. It invited audiences at The Market Theatre (and across its American and British tours) to reflect on their complicity in, or proximity to, the everyday realities of state repression alongside the appalling instances of violence encountered by Black and Coloured South Africans and those who fought alongside them against oppression.

Beyond standing as a illustrative example of a Living Newspaper emerging in a period of crisis – and a context of media suppression – this case study also fruitfully pushes at the boundaries of the Living Newspaper, underscoring its relationship with other forms that deploy the real. As Sarah Roberts identifies, *Born in the RSA* is a significant work in apartheid era drama and has been variously described as docu-drama, a Living Newspaper, and a work that 'explicitly crystallized the notion of theatre as testimony' (Roberts, 2015: 63).[4] Out of the case studies explored in this Element, this play in particular illuminates

[4] Frank Rich, theatre critic at the New York Times, speaks to the formal fluidity that surrounded *Born in the RSA*, noting that '[t]he simple format has less in common with our own theater's Depression-era "Living Newspapers" than with latter-day English documentary plays by David Hare (Fanshen) and Caryl Churchill (Fen)' (Rich, 1986: 3). Rich's comment is indicative of the ways in which the Living Newspaper has become synonymous with the Federal Theatre Project, a history which we hope this book contributes to decentring.

the ways in which Living Newspapers sits productively alongside documentary performance and theatre of testimony. In situating *Born in the RSA* as a Living Newspaper we underline the ways in which it utilises modes synonymous with broader lineages of the form: a collage of dialogue, direct address, media projections, song, and choreography. Beyond this, exploring the play through a lens of newspaper aesthetics exposes three elements that are key to our conceptualisation of the Living Newspaper: 1) the importance of research practices that attend to diverse and multiple narratives in the process of producing a performance; 2) the strategies of montage and narrative that the form offers to move beyond individual verbatim accounts to a collective and fictionalised representation of communities lived realities; 3) and the way the form is shaped by how the media functions within the context of its production.

Simon blends 'techniques of journalism and theatre' to tell the stories of the seven characters (Osofisan, 2001: 160). These characters were composite, created from the actors own personal experiences and their extensive documentary research. In the programme note for *Born in the RSA*, Simon explained that the performers researched in libraries; spoke with activists who had been incarcerated; spent time with political lawyer Priscilla Jana; visited the office of a detainees committee that was tasked with supporting parents to find children arrested by the state (Gray, 1990). The process utilised for *Born in the RSA* foregrounds the rigorous research that underpins many approaches to the Living Newspaper. Whether it's by journalists employed by the Federal Theatre Project in 1930s USA or by performers themselves as in this example – the form demands a careful attention to and excavation of the narratives that appear (or are occluded from) the news. Further the performance itself asserts the contradictory, conflicting, and competing narratives that operate through the media and in performance.

Simon's approach of workshopping performer-led research coupled with encouraging performers to situate themselves within the context of the play produced a nuanced presentation of their real encounters through a fictional frame. Reflecting on Simon's methodology, Yvette Hutchinson acknowledges he created

> space for expression of diverse 'truths', without needing or wanting to direct the narratives [which] made him an extraordinary culture-broker, who by not intervening in the process or product offered the opportunity for significant broader cultural intervention and change. (Hutchinson, 2003: 13)

Simon's approach to theatremaking as a montage of experiences, research, and responsivity to the environment resonates with the histories of Living Newspapers and illuminates the cultural potential of the form to offer a space for multiplicity, critique and exchange. Roberts has asserted the significance of montage within Simon's practice during this period, as it 'constitut[es] a 'social or dialogic truth': no single individual account could lay greater claim or insight to the South African experience than any other' (Roberts, 2015: 23). The Living Newspaper form, in both its layering of perspectives and its varied performance modes, holds space for these complexities to emerge and remain unresolved.

Beyond the montage approach that *Born in the RSA* illuminates, the play also underscores the multifaceted relationship between the real and the fictional that is a central interplay within Living Newspapers. As Federal Theatre playwright Arthur Arendt expressed,

> The living newspaper is a dramatization of a problem composed in greater or lesser extent of many news events, all bearing on the one subject and interlarded with typical but non-factual representations of the effect of these news events on the people to whom the problem is of great importance. (Arendt in Bradby and McCormick, 1978: 22)

The use of 'typical but non-factual representations', is significant as a way to distinguish Living Newspapers from documentary or testimonial forms, with this use of the 'typical' as a device through which to examine the systemic as well as reflect on individual experiences of a context. Hutchinson has noted, *Born in the RSA* 'is a fictional narrative, but in many ways its 'feasibility' is as striking as any documented text may have been, and it forces one to hear it in relation to oneself' (2009: 216). The creative frame of the Living Newspaper offers a different mode through which to attend to the interviews, observations, and lived experiences being explored in the work. Simon's approach highlights the broader intermingling of fiction and fact which is a central aspect of Living Newspapers, which is often under explored in critical engagements with the form. The research and responsivity that underpins this form is consistently coupled with a fictional frame, which varies in approach, but which holds the tension between the real and the imagined in a way that often confronts the audience. Given Living Newspaper's attention to their political context and an engagement with the news of the day, in a context of censorship a dramaturgy that enabled a coming together of real experiences with fictional strategies and aesthetic frames, was vital.

Across the play the seven characters utilise direct address, predominantly in the past tense, to narrate the events of the play. Drawing on Simon's previous experiments with narrative strategies synonymous with epic theatre in *Black Dog* (1984), this device of retelling makes up much of *Born in the RSA*'s content with vignettes of scenes between characters interspersed throughout. For example, Zachariah's monologue upon seeing young Dumisani beaten body,

> Mia answered the door herself.
>
> Can I see him?' We tiptoed down the passage and stopped at a door. She opened it Dumisani was lying on his back in a big double bed. His face was swollen, his eyes closed. Everything around him was little blue flowers. The curtains. The wallpaper. The cushion under his head. He started moaning and Mia quickly closed the door . . .
>
> I just wanted to pick him up and carry him home. (Simon, 1997)

The language of the play is itself journalistic with characters reporting events to the audience. Indeed, the technique of verbalising the most egregious harm characters endured stood in for violence being enacted onstage, emphasising the power of speaking these narratives to audiences rather than restaging the violence. In contrast to a docu-drama, which focuses on the 'real' experiences of the individual being portrayed, the Living Newspaper's expansive fictional frame and montage approach enables work to engage with a collective politics. In his monologue Zachariah continues,

> I walked back towards the bus stop. I realized that I was still carrying his baseball bat and recorder. As I passed the convent school I was still thinking of Dumisani. The playground was full of little white girls in their neat uniforms having their morning break. I watched them running, laughing, and playing [. . .]. I thought, ja, every one of you has a nanny. She feeds you, she comforts you, she washes that uniform, she polishes those shoes, and every time she leaves Soweto or Alexandra and says goodbye to her own children, she doesn't know whether she'll see them again, alive or dead. Ja, your nanny knows where your kitchen knives are [. . .]. Your mommy's nanny knew too. But how many of you do they kill? Ask about her children, and the soldiers who shoot them dead. Ask her what she's waiting for? For us to prove that we can kill children as well as they can? (Simon, 1997)

The Living Newspaper is rooted in the contemporary lived realities of the communities and landscapes it depicts without being necessarily tied to the story of specific individuals. In the context of *Born in the RSA* Zachariah then, is able to both speak to a collective encounter with injustice that is representative of a broader struggle and voice the unspeakable.

> Suddenly I move through the gates to the middle of the playground. I started to swing the baseball bat – skulls cracked – brains and baby teeth flew [. . .]. I was a panther, I was a tiger, I was everything they wanted me to be. I was their black King Kong. A bell started to ring. I found myself on the pavement. The bell was calling the children to go inside. I continued to watch them play. I couldn't breathe. I turned and started walking up Oxford Road. I heard myself yelling Fuck you! Fuck you! Fuck you for what you have done to Dumisani and fuck you fuck you fuck you for what you are doing to me! (Simon, 1997)

Here Zachariah's violent fantasy underscores the distinction between the value of white children and Black children that operated under apartheid and amplifies the brutality of Dumisani's beating at the hands of the state. The form importantly is not simply reporting the facts but, through satire and distorted events, exposes the opaque realities of living under apartheid. *Born in the RSA* underscores the political potential of holding the fictional, and the fantastical, in tension with the real in performance.

The play illuminates specific practices of the Living Newspaper that position it as particularly resonant during a period of crisis. at As Amlin Gray wrote in a programme note to accompany the production in the USA,

> Perhaps only in a time of crisis can Simon's montage method work so powerfully. Determined commitment and pure accident can embroil any individual in South Africa's upheavals, as they embroil *RSA's* wider range of characters. Simon and his actors found their subjects in the life around them. [. . .] In the fear-struck silence that attends much of life in South Africa. (Gray, 1990: 7)

This approach to the Living Newspaper – its use of montage, direct address and narration, and nuanced intermingling of the real and fiction – becomes more urgent during a period in which media censorship is pervasive. The multiple voices and narratives that the Living Newspaper form facilitates are particularly well positioned to speak to crisis, in this instance a crisis that prohibited its own articulation. The mode of montage and the device of 'typical but non-factual representations' can sufficiently hold the experience of crisis, which is an assemblage of contradictions, oppressions, and ambiguities.

Newspaper Theatre: A Tool for Creative Agency

While *Born in the RSA* sought to stage citizens reporting the realities of living in South Africa in the 1980s, *Teatro Jornal* aimed to foster citizens participation in critiquing and performing the news under the military dictatorship (which operated from 1964 to 1985) in Brazil. There are strong formal and political resonances between Living Newspapers and, what Augusto Boal termed, *Teatro Jornal* (Newspaper Theatre). As Frances Babbage has identified, Boal's body of work was informed by a diverse range of practices within and beyond South America, including overlaps with practices of the Living Newspaper (2004: 32). Newspaper Theatre was foundational to what would later become Theatre of the Oppressed and was initially developed by the Nucleus Group of the Teatro de Arena in São Paulo, prior to Boal's imprisonment in 1971 and subsequent exile. Newspaper Theatre emerged in Brazil as a response to absences, erasures and politically motivated misrepresentations present within the media due to significant restrictions on freedom of speech under the military dictatorship. Writing on the development of Newspaper Theatre as a model of practice Boal notes,

> The primary objective of Newspaper Theatre is to devolve theatre to the people. The secondary objective is to attempt to demystify the pretended 'objectivity' of most journalism, to show that all news published in the paper is a work of fiction at the service of the dominant class. (Boal, 1998: 192)

Newspaper Theatre sought to both intervene in delineations between 'artists' and 'the people', positioning the latter as 'creative agents'. It also aimed to instil a criticality in the ways in which people engage with news and its underlying politics, particularly given the use of the media as a tool within the military dictatorship. In this section, we engage with Newspaper Theatre to reflect on the political potential of a community theatre that engages with the news during a period of crisis.

Boal developed eleven principles of Newspaper Theatre that communities could use to develop creative theatrical responses to contemporary events. These principles offer a comprehensive and tangible set of tools for people to develop engaged and critical responses to the news through performance.

1. Simple Reading
2. Complementary Reading
3. The Crossed Reading
4. The Rhythmical Reading
5. The Reinforced Reading
6. The Parallel Action
7. The Historical Reading
8. Improvisation
9. The Concretion of Abstraction
10. Text Out of Context
11. Insertion into the Actual Context (Boal, 1998: 194–201)

In critically reflecting on newspaper aesthetics and Kondo's conceptualisation of worldmaking through theatre as 'reparative creativity', we argue that Boal's model can be grouped into three tenets: Placement, Omission, and Exposing 'the real'. We propose that each of these tenets is formally significant in a broader framework of the Living Newspaper, and other theatre practices rooted in the news.

The first of these – Placement – focuses on developing a critical attention to the underpinning ideologies that inform layout and positioning in news media. *Simple Reading* invites people to read a news item aloud without comment, in order to isolate the story from its given layout within newspaper (e.g. front page and full spread or buried in the middle in a side column). The sparseness of this approach, Boal proposes, offers an opportunity to peel back any surrounding artifice or coding placed on the story and see it afresh. *Crossed Reading*, similarly focuses on the positioning of narratives proposing holding two different news stories together, cross cutting them in a way that one illuminates the politics of another. More broadly, Newspaper Theatre asks participants to contextualise (and relocate) the placement of events within a wider global history – *Historical Reading* – or within a different context – *Text out of Context*, which might apply to a relocation of site or of linguistic style. These dramaturgical and critical approaches to storytelling are a key aspect of newspaper aesthetics and find their echo in Simon's use of montage in *Born in the RSA*. In attending to both the literal position in which a story appears in a newspaper and that story's relation to its site, time, and style, Newspaper Theatre unfurls the ways in which placement within a newspaper – or within the news cycle and digital dissemination of news – is imbued with politics both in the media and in the events it covers. Encouraging makers to attend to placement critically offers productive potential for political theatre making. Indeed, this engagement with placement is a central tenet of the Royal Court's *A Counter Narrative*, which we discuss as later in this section.

Omission is the second core element of our framing of Newspaper Theatre; as Boal notes in his description of the practice, 'Sometimes, the lack of a word or a phrase gives a particular slant to the reality presented; in this case the news is not false, it is incomplete, and, by this means, the way the news item will be received is adulterated, and reality is deformed' (Boal, 1998: 195). Three of the eleven principles of Newspaper Theatre directly address this deformation of reality: *Complementary Reading, Concretion of Abstraction,* and *Insertion into the Actual Context.* The first takes up newspaper articles and adds in relevant data, narratives, or people who have been elided from stories in order to give a fuller picture of events. *Concretion of Abstraction*, seeks to find affective modes to communicate the reality of a story 'discovering which live images are capable of making certain dead or worn-out words real in a way they have not been' (Boal, 1998: p.244). *Insertion into the Actual Context* seeks to move beyond individual stories and provoke people to explore wider systems and power structures that shape our experiences. These three approaches seek to use performance to ignite the affective, relational, and material realties of news stories that have been obscured. They are intended to move audiences closer to the lived experience of the news and in doing so assert the specific value of performance as a mode of engaging with the news during a period when its legitimacy is in crisis.

As explored in relation to *Born in the RSA*, the blurring of reality and fiction is a central tension held by theatre practice engaging with the news. Boal proposes a range of different semiotic modes in order to reveal an underlying truth in reporting: *Rhythmical Reading*, the use of song, poetry, or repetition to 'filter' the news and expose its reality; inspired by advertising strategies *Reinforced Reading* uses slogans, images, slides, or jingles to promote key messages; and in *Improvising,* the news becomes stimulus to explore creatively and in doing so to experiment and investigate the situation live through different iterations. While Simon's work utilises a fictional frame to expose South Africans everyday experiences in 1985, Boal's approach to the blurring between fact and fiction is rooted in a critique of the fictionalisation of the news under the military dictatorship and the use of performance strategies as a way to reveal the obscured truth of the stories told. Through Rhythmical Reading, Reinforced Reading, and Improvising, Newspaper Theatre performs and makes explicit the gap between the reported story and the reality. Exposing the real, therefore, is an approach to illuminating the gap between the real and the news, which underscores the ways in which the news becomes a tool to maintain oppression.

Boal and his collaborators at the Teatro de Arena developed a structured model of practice for non-professional performers to engage with the news through theatre. Historically, the Living Newspaper had made both the news and performance more widely accessible: in Russia in the 1920s, then in China and the USA in the 1930s, this practice brought performance to the streets, the factories, and the front lines, communicating the news to different audiences. As we have asserted, Newspaper Theatre draws from resonant principles of Placement, Omission, and Exposing 'the real'; but it moves beyond presenting publics with newspaper aesthetics and invites them to participate in creating and deploying those aesthetics as tools to interrogate the news and the worlds it constructs.

Engaging with Newspaper as Form

The Royal Court's *Living Newspaper: A Counter Narrative* explicitly engaged with the plurality of *written forms* deployed in newspapers, using these stylistic modes as both stimulus and holding framework for the pieces produced as part of the project. Each edition consisted of a range of performance works that directly aligned with forms of writing that appear in the newspaper: the front page, long look or long listen (a take on the long read), cartoon, weather, horoscope, dating, subverts (a take on adverts), agony aunt, obituaries, and the news stand – a flexible section that 'allows a number of smaller articles to take place'(Royal Court, 2020).[5] As well as the performances themselves, the Royal Court produced a zine to accompany each issue. The zines categorise the performance pieces under the following headings:

Cartoon: A space for satire through the lens of the cartoon. Realised through cut-outs, speech bubbles, timber and fixed objects made in the scenery dock each week.
Weather Room: An installation designed to evoke changing weather dates. A space to contemplate our own impact on the climate crisis.
Long Look: a kit formed from physical frames laid out in a number of ways to tell a multitude of visual stories/ Long Listen: a relaxed space allowing an audience a chance to pause and engage with a longer piece of writing.
Agony Aunt: A chance for audiences to seek advice, confess and be heard with each week's Agony Auntie behind a screen in a private booth.
Obituary: This section forms a long procession down the main front of house staircase. This is a site to remember, reminisce and rejoice in the memory of people, places and things that may have been lost this year which accumulates over the six weeks.
Royal Courting: As if love has thrown up in the bar. A space to congregate and witness as a new love blossoms each week in real life, far from swiping right in dating apps.
Subverts: Subversive advertising, delivered through quick, gestural inventions using a range of communication styles and ideas. Found in stairways, corridors and other transitional spaces. (Royal Court, 2020)

The Royal Court therefore constructed specific frames around each form – both spatially and in terms of aesthetic modes – offering their own model for translating newspaper to the stage. Again, there are strong resonances between this montage approach and Simon's approach at the Market Theatre. The scale and format of *A Counter Narrative* (seven editions, each with ten short pieces of new writing) is reliant on a montage strategy that produces multiple perspectives, responses, and readings of the news each week. A significant aspect of the project is its documentation of tens of playwrights' and hundreds of creatives' critical responses to the news at the close of 2020 and across 2021.

A Counter Narrative also aligns with principles of Newspaper Theatre, in the project's keen attention to the placement, style, and layout of the newspaper as a document and how that is made manifest in performance. This attention to the different modalities of how stories are communicated in the media echoes

[5] In addition, there were several holding frameworks that were specifically anchored in the site of the theatre itself: substage, a blank space, and the control room – we will discuss these site-based pieces in Section 4.

Boal's attention to what stories get told in particular forms and inviting us to consider what that form reveals about the status or significance of particular narratives. *A Counter Narrative* experimented with the politics of specific forms of writing within newspapers, utilising The Front Page to connote the central focus of each issue and playing with an exploration of weighty topics through more marginal modes such as the subverts or the obituaries. Utilising these identifiable modes of journalistic writing offers a sustained intervention into the form of the Living Newspaper, foregrounding the ways in which we package and consume news in a way that invites critique of the structures and dissemination of news itself as well as the content of the works. This approach was also a provocation to playwrights to think through what that written form might look like as a 'living' performance practice. Where earlier iterations of Living Newspapers (e.g. Federal Theatre Project, Blue Blouses etc.) have focused on how the content of the news might be animated in performance, *A Counter Narrative* underscores the departure evident in newspaper aesthetics of the late twentieth and early twenty-first century in its consideration of what the hierarchies and politics of forms of writing might offer performance.

The playwrights and creative teams (who changed across each edition of the project) could then experiment within the given structure of staging the newspaper. Indeed the editions demonstrate the diversity of aesthetic approaches writers projected onto the frames given by the Royal Court. The Obituaries – a particularly pertinent site of exploration during the COVID-19 pandemic – shift in style, length, and cast size across each edition as playwrights offer different approaches to examine death, grief, and loss. Emteaz Hussain's protagonist in *Strawberries* (Edition Two) relays the story of Jen, a young woman being moved out of a women's refuge in order to make room for a mother with children; failed by those she seeks support from Jen commits suicide. *Obituary* by Leo Butler (Edition Three), deploys a television news format with presenter Helen Peacock announcing the death of 'Debate and Nuance', with an accompanying critique of the contemporary political context of the UK: 'Boris Johnson announced that Debate's corpse will be glued to the side of a double decker bus as part of the Festival of Brexit. Alas, no such honour for Nuance who last night unfortunately took her own life while being held at Brook House Detention Centre' (Butler, 2021). In monologue *Eulogy for a Dead Life* (Edition Four) Gurpreet Kaur Bhatti explores the difficulties of mourning a cruel father, alluding to how the complicated relationship makes this loss and its impact deeply complicated. Indicative of the range across all seven editions, the obituary section oscillated between aching personal losses, the death of collectively held values, and ailing support systems, forms of community, and safety nets. By taking up the mode of obituary in this way *A Counter Narrative*, and the playwrights involved, provoke a reflection on the function of public mourning and collective memorialisation that this register of writing performs. Further, in a period of a significant increase in deaths and an experience of global grieving, Hussain, Bhatti, and Butler's works enables a layered examination of what is being lost in this moment and what has long been ailing.

While the Obituary offered a written form that playwrights could mould to address the contemporary moment, other newspaper forms presented a particular challenge to the modes of communication most regularly utilised by playwrights. As writer Mark Ravenhill reflects on his own experience writing a Cartoon,

> You sort of question 'Why am I writing a description for a cartoon? That's an entirely visual thing.' But I guess as a writer, you are always training yourself to think visually as well as through words. I think most of us do have 'stage pictures' in our heads as we write and the most satisfying theatre is that meeting of the text and the image. So yeah, that felt particularly weird as well as the fact that it had to be like a cartoon you'd have in a newspaper, so it should also be very hot-off-the-press. (Ravenhill, 2021)

Sami Ibrahim's Cartoon for Edition Three *The Foreign Invasion – Or – Mr Johnson Taking Control of Things* restages eighteenth-century caricaturist James Gillray's 'The French invasion; – or – John Bull, bombarding the bum-boats', which shows all of the counties of England in the figure of John Bull (a personification of the nation) defecating on invading French ships. In a two minute sketch, Ibrahim's piece depicts the construction of a contemporary iteration of this cartoon with a performer portraying (then Prime Minster) Boris Johnson as the central figure gradually dressing himself with a series of foam counties of England, ultimately affixing a map of the country on his body. As the performer adorns himself in each of the counties a voiceover relays the history of Gillray's cartoon and articulates its resonance with an England that pursues damaging isolationist policies in relation to immigration (the Hostile Environment) and international collaboration (Brexit)[6]:

> Big or small, we can handle any invader.
> Napoleon? Fuck off back to France
> Hitler? Fuck off back to Germany
> The EU? Fuck off back to Brussels
> Covid? Fuck off back to China
> Migrants? Fuck off back to wherever you came from.

[6] This piece was created in 2021 but, illustrative of its relevance in contemporary Britain, at the time of writing in 2023 MP and deputy chairman of the Conservative Party, Lee Anderson, publicly stated migrants should 'fuck off back to France' if they are unhappy with British immigration processes (Maddox, 2023). Anderson was tacitly supported by the government in his expression of this sentiment.

> [. . .]
> We'll shit on ourselves if we have to
> We aren't afraid: any threat – from anywhere – and any angle – at any point.
> We know what to do.
> *Then the map does a big, explosive, long lasting shit.*
> We know how to take control.

The invitation to write a cartoon for stage invokes a particular aesthetic. Ibrahim engaged with the register of visual satire that the cartoon form invites, along with bright and bold scenographic choices. Further, Ibrahim draws on a history of newspaper cartoon satire, utilising a live performer to animate this contemporary reworking cartoon. In Edition One, Nazareth Hassan's *Cartoon of The Week* staged an interactive caricature with the scene dock decked in American flags, toy tanks and soldiers, food and toilet rolls with a Trump figure at its centre. The single performer portraying an American Republican then encouraged the audience (who were present in person at this edition) to fill in speech bubbles attached to the figures of 'Generic American Guy', 'Twin 1' and 'Twin 2'. Audiences shout out responses including 'QAnon is my Daddy' and 'The Virus is a lie' to be filled into the speech bubbles. The participatory mode of Hassan's cartoon illuminates the collective language of the cartoon satire. Holding Hassan and Ibrahim's responses together illuminates the different modes through which performance can utilise cartoon as stimulus and animate this form through live performance. The Cartoon and the Obituary illuminate a distinctive aspect of *A Counter Narrative*, the ways in which the project which staged the shapes, languages, and practices of the newspaper for its audiences. In so doing it offered a reflection on the news as a mode of world making, asking: what are the frames and forms through which we communicate stories in the media and how does this shape our understanding of these stories?

Conclusion

In this section, we have identified and examined newspaper aesthetics, specifically those present in theatre practices from South Africa, South America, and the UK in order to both underscore the ways in which such performance engages in worldmaking to foster critique within periods of crisis and highlight how the dramaturgies of this work are *shaped by* the crisis it occupies. Across the three examples explored here we have demonstrated the rich variety of practices that sit within newspaper aesthetics (documentary, community, new writing) and explored the range of strategies used in these areas to navigate differing economic and political contexts (montage, gathering testimony, engaging participants in critical readings of the news, experiments with staging printed forms). Foregrounding of a multiplicity of experiences, a radical resistance to censorship, and a fierce critique of dominant hierarchies (of power, of form) are also core to our conceptualisation of Living Newspaper. We have illuminated the ways in which theatre makers engaged with the news to expose the social, economic, and political nature of its construction. Further, in different ways Simon, Boal, and the creatives involved in *A Counter Narrative*, staged the processes of making and remaking local, national, and global narratives that are played out in the news media. In all three examples, building on Kondo, we have demonstrated how artists have sought to remake and repair the worlds which their work occupies – in these acts of worldmaking such performance has the capacity to show the resonances and disjunctures between lived experiences and media narratives.

3 Site Specific Meets Digital Theatre: The Living Newspaper as Mediated Performance

Performance artist Nando Messias sits on the white stone steps in front of the Royal Court Theatre, dressed in a black gown, jewelled necklace, thick pale blue shawl, and red elbow length gloves. Behind Messias and occupying the backdrop of the frame are the building's glass front doors that lead into the theatre box office; long emblazoned with the words 'COME IN' in bright white block capitals. Messias stands, walks directly towards the viewer, and opens their black clutch bag pulling out a bunch of theatre tickets with the Royal Court embossing. The tickets have been scrawled on in black pen and Messias presents them to the camera, gradually unfurling them to read: 'Please come back'/'I don't know who I am'/without you'. The tickets are presented one by one, Messias cycling through them for viewers to read 'I know'/'You Don't feel safe'/'W me'. Messias then returns to sit on the steps, then holds up several cardboard placards: 'Want you here'/'Want you in me'/'us'/ 'Even in bits'. Again, Messias descends the steps, moving towards the camera. Pulling a phone from their clutch they type notes and show them one by one to the viewer: 'don't know if I need you anymore'/'im lying'/'can you hear me'/'do you want to smell me, and see me, and be in me'/'or not'/'?'/'Going so dark'/'where r u'. Messias then returns the phone to their bag and removes one red glove to reveal black marker on their arm reading: 'My wounded love', then turning to the inside of their arm: 'Come home' and opening their palm: 'You still got keys'. Pulling down the front of their dress Messias then writes on their chest: 'Door is always open'. They turn, drop their shawl off their shoulders to reveal across their back: 'House is open'. Messias then ascends the stairs and disappears into the theatre, the writing across their back calling us to join them.

Edition Six of the Royal Court's *A Counter Narrative* was released at the start of May 2021 just weeks ahead of 17 May, when UK theatre buildings were allowed to fully reopen for the first time since their closure in March 2020. In Hester Chillingworth's *Mi Casa es Su Casa*, Messias embodies the theatre building yearning to be occupied again while also acknowledging the anxieties of audiences to return to sites of collective gathering, and the ongoing challenges faced by bringing people together. The different strategies of presenting writing (on tickets, on placards, on a phone, on bodies) echoes the Court's position as a writing focused venue, mirroring the multiple approaches to inviting audiences back that theatres were taking in this moment. Throughout *Mi Casa es Su Casa* the materiality of the building and audiences' experiences of it – through smell, touch, sight – is asserted and the vitality of collective gathering to theatre's functioning is underscored.

Given the centrality of negotiating site to Living Newspapers, in this section we consider how the form might be productively reconstituted when theatre spaces and buildings are in crisis. We take up Fintan Walsh's examination of crisis, in his work on troubled and troubling masculinities, which reasserts the potentiality of crisis:

> discourses of crisis rarely concede to the condition's reconstitutive dimension. In place of this presumption of stasis, or failure, I suggest that crisis is not an end in itself but a period of disorder that precedes and precipitates a longer period of productivity, restructuring, and redevelopment, which may even lead to the reestablishment of the temporarily agitated norm. (Walsh, 2010: 8)

Crisis then might be understood as a space of opportunity wherein established norms are agitated and different futures are envisaged. Returning to crisis management scholarship, t' Hart's conceptualisation of crisis resonates with this framing, asserting that in such periods,

> The fact that certain aspects of the old order are delegitimised opens up opportunities for rallying people behind visions of a new order, or at least to solicit mass support for measures that can be depicted as 'lessons' for the 'improvement' of the old order. (1993: 40)

Crisis becomes productive, to an extent, through delegitimising the norms that preceded and, to a greater or lesser extent, precipitated it. The persistent appearance of Living Newspapers during periods of crisis locate it as a fertile tool through which to generate these visions of a new order, to understand and interrogate lessons from the past, or to critique the existing status quo. In this section, we particularly examine how a turn to Living Newspaper offers a distinctive insight into the interplay between the material site and the mediated experience in performance and consider how various crises have invoked a desire for a new kind of theatre to emerge.

The importance of site in the mass dissemination of Living Newspapers has persisted across its history. We begin with a focus on Russia in the 1920s, where the emergence of this form was initially premised on reaching mass audiences through performances on the front lines of war, and later in public spaces, factories, and workers clubs. We then turn to a case study of UK-based community arts organisation C&T to reflect on how their initiation of digital Living Newspapers resonates with its historical practices of mediation and reorients the form's relationship to physical spaces. Finally, we examine how the materiality of the Royal Court building manifested at live in person performances and how the centrality of the theatre building was translated in digitally disseminated performances. Across our analysis we identify how, as a form, the Living Newspaper supports an engagement with mediated communication and digital practice in ways that do not occlude the materiality of sites of performance.

Soviet Russia and the Blue Blouse Movement

As we touched on in the Introduction, Living Newspapers – *zhivaia gazeta* – were first devised in Soviet Russia and utilised by the Bolsheviks during the Russian Civil War (1918–1920) to disseminate political messages to the predominantly illiterate troops of the Red Army. This built on previous practices of oral newspaper in Russia, where the newspaper would be read aloud in public spaces in order to disseminate the news of the day – and its political underpinnings – to the working-class population. The Living Newspaper, dramatized these readings and began utilising modes such as satire, verse, and song. During the civil war theatre troupes toured the front lines of the conflict and performed pro-Bolshevik Living Newspapers to the soldiers. In 1920 alone over a thousand theatre troupes performed for the Red Army and the form was established as its own distinct practice in these tours of the front lines (Senelick, 2014).

Following the Bolshevik victory, Living Newspapers continued to gain traction, expanding beyond the battlefields to the streets, workers clubs, and workplaces. The government provided significant economic and cultural support for Living Newspapers that underpinned their expansion across Russia. The most significant collective utilising this form was the Blue Blouse Movement (*Siniaia bluza*), named for the basic blue workers' shirts that performers wore, who were founded in 1923 by Boris Yuzhanin with the backing of the Moscow School of Journalism. Yuzhanin and the avant-garde playwrights who collaborated on Blue Blouse performances drew on 'lit montage', wherein scripts comprised of reworkings and mash ups of material from newspapers, magazines, and government documentation. The Moscow Blue Blouse troupe were soon incorporated into the Moscow trade union organisation and operated under the cultural wing of the union as a professional performance troupe, producing their own journal *Sinyaya Bluza* to disseminate their aesthetic manifesto and publish playtexts. The popularity and accessibility of the form resulted in amateur companies taking up the Living Newspaper and by the late 1920s the Blue Blouse movement consisted of nearly 5,000 companies with nearly 100,000 members, predominantly within Russia but also beyond its borders (Mally, 2008). This positioned the form as significant in the cultural, political, and economic life of Russia in the 1920s. Blue Blouse established a set of performance strategies that would serve as foundational to the Living Newspaper as a form – a parade of 'headlines' followed by a montage of satirical skits, monologues, dance, mime, acrobatics, and songs. However, by the early 1930s state support for Living Newspapers began to wane and as Lynn Mally notes in 1932 'the Soviet government summarily shut down most cultural organizations that claimed special ties to the proletariat. Instead, state cultural agencies began to foster art forms that would appeal beyond the urban working class' (Mally, 2008: 7). This reflected the turn away from forms framed as avant-garde by the government, which accompanied the Stalinist industrialization drive of the late twenties and early thirties. State cultural policy during this time prioritized social realism and more singular and didactic forms of agitprop.

Site shaped the aesthetics of the Living Newspaper, given its emergence in theatre troupes touring the front line and its establishment in 1920s Russia as performance created for public spaces and industrial workplaces. In the first edition of the *Sinyaya Bluza journal* Novitsky, head of the Artistic Division of the Glavnauka, outlines ten characteristics of Blue Blouse with the third being 'The "Blue Blouse" is a versatile, living, juicy, bright, portable itinerant form that can work in any public space under any conditions' (Novitsky in Senelick, 2014). Blue Blouse aesthetics were underpinned by the intention that performance should be portable. As Mally has noted, due to the nature of performances being staged in the streets, clubs, or factories, Living Newspapers rarely had any set, 'To get their messages across to audiences, they used exaggerated props, very simple costumes, and a variety of posters, flags, and slides' (2008: 6). There was an urgency to communicate to as wide an audience as possible through creating touring work with bold semiotics that would work in 'any conditions'. This urgency in communication and use of amplified scenographic choices can be traced through its various subsequent iterations of Living Newspapers, even those which have occurred in theatre venues.

While the ability of the form to succeed anywhere is important, Novitsky's articulation of the key characteristics of Blue Blouse goes beyond this, also asserting the *specificity* of the place in which Living Newspapers flourished most:

> 4. The 'Blue Blouse' is a club, cabaret form, a special aspect of amateur artistic work in worker's clubs. It was born spontaneously and in the clubs has supplanted the bourgeois play, 'insularity', and amateurishness. (Novitsky in Senelick, 2014)

The Living Newspaper was produced for venues outside of theatre buildings; site was vital but, in the Blue Blouse and early examples of the form, the site was explicitly not the traditional theatre space. The Living Newspaper flourished in workers clubs alongside the cabaret scene, affirming the working class proliferation of the form. The club site was important as it was both a venue for Blue Blouse troupes to perform and also served as a meeting space for amateur creators to gather and produce their own Living Newspapers. Acknowledging the importance of clubs illuminates the form as an accessible one, through which people can meet and create in response to the news of the day, although this practice of production as a mode of resistance became more legible in later Living Newspaper projects (e.g. Augusto Boal's *Teatro Jornal*). Additionally, underscoring the history of the Living Newspaper as club performance situates it in a lineage of radical popular performance. The foundational aesthetics of the form were shaped by the public sites (workers club, town square, and factories) it initially occupied.

C&T Networked Participation and Creating Theatricality Digitally

C&T are a UK-based applied theatre company that draw on creative technologies to work with communities in different global contexts. Founded in Worcester (England) in 1988 as a theatre in education company by Paul Sutton, Andy Sheard, Martin Felton, and Liz Stone, since the mid 1990s the company has foregrounded creative technology and digital practices in their work. They now work all over the world, with ongoing partnerships in Kenya, Australia, the USA, and New Zealand, and are at the forefront of participatory digital theatre experiences. In the early 1990s C&T began to experiment with the Living Newspaper as a form and this was significant to the company's development of projects that operated across networks of participants in different locations and their increasing interest in exploring how theatre might engage with mediation (in terms of how processes and politics of communication shape and circulate meaning). As Sutton asserts, 'an underpinning strand of all of C&T's work is about how vocabulary of theatre and performance allows you to dissect mediated forms of communication', the Living Newspaper was a locus of development for these ideas (Sutton, P, Zoom interview with authors, 28 March 2023). Turning to this case study exposes that, while material sites have historically been integral to the Living Newspaper, as a form implicitly concerned with the mediated it is uniquely placed to explore the interplay between physical and digital spaces in performance.

The company's engagement with the form of the Living Newspaper began in 1995 when they were tasked to create a community play with unemployed young people in Worcester. C&T felt that the Living Newspaper would be a prescient form to enable young people, who had been disenfranchised and marginalised, to feel a sense of agency over the stories they were telling. There was a keenness to help young people to challenge the ways in which they were being represented in mainstream narratives, 'that they [C&T and the participants they engaged] perceived as being actively trying to undermine the values and interests of young, young people' (Sutton, P, Zoom interview with authors, 28 March 2023). The project therefore sought to equip participants with the skills to critique dominant discourses, particularly pervasive negative depictions of young people. In this context, the Living Newspaper was a performance mode that enabled participants '[t]o dissect the world events, understand the process of editorial decision making and editorial values, [. . .] it was about the subversion and the deconstructed mainstream media messages' (Sutton, P, Zoom interview with authors, 28 March 2023). Resonant with Paul t' Hart's assertion that crises delegitimise the old-world order, the content and form of crisis theatre seeks to disrupt existing narratives and offer new alternatives (t' Hart, 1993). Finding ways to critically engage young people during a period of persistently high youth unemployment offers the potential to challenge the hegemonic representations of them in the mainstream. For C&T, the process of creating the Living Newspapers therefore became as much a core an element of the work as the performances themselves, with the form supporting the development of critical skills in deciphering and speaking back to messages young people encountered in the mainstream media.

The initial iteration of C&T's Living Newspaper project created eight live performances over a two-year period working with a shifting group of involved fifty young people in Worcester. The work was facilitated by C&T practitioners in collaboration with a journalist, to support the critical development of the young people in media practices. This first cycle of the project opened with the young people involved collaborating in a workshop space together. The participants undertook a group brainstorming exercise on newspaper end roll and were asked to write down the things that annoyed or angered them, filling the paper with topics and themes. Once the roll was filled, the group would review all the areas and each individual young person had a number of votes to allocate to areas they wanted to explore. Through this iterative process the initial brainstorm was then refined down to a common set of themes and areas, which the group would then explore and find common connecting lines across them. This exercise supported the participants to create a kind of shared editorial policy for their approach to media and their own presentation of it. C&T staged seven separate Living Newspaper performances. The project then culminated with an eighth immersive performance, *Hump Shunted* (1997), created by 80 young people between the ages of eight and twenty, staged in a disused cinema. Well preceding the Brexit referendum of 2016, *Hump Shunted* depicted young people's perspective on Britain's place in Europe since World War Two and focused on the tensions within the nation's relationship to the continent.

The Living Newspaper has always been a mediated form, which has drawn on slides, image and film projections, utilising the cross cutting of live and mediated signifiers since its inception. While this first iteration of the C&T project was created and presented in live spaces, Sutton asserts the significance of recognising the work as mediated while operating in a live space:

> as with classic Living Newspapers, we were using slide projections. But we were still back in the days of clunky old carousel slide projectors and photographs and things like that. [...] We were editing videos but it was in much more of a complex time-consuming process and we were projecting those on big screens in spaces. That was pretty high-tech stuff back then. But there was that sense of it as a mixed media experience. But clearly, we were developing something that was a form of mediated performance. (Sutton, P, Zoom interview with authors, 28 March 2023)

Sutton underscores the need to understand all Living Newspapers as mediated, due to its use of a montage of modes of communication and its implicit reflection on mediatisation in its content and form. Given this historical attachment to the media and the mediated, the Living Newspaper then, has always productively dissolved the binaries between theatre buildings and mediated performance.

The next iteration of the Living Newspaper at C&T in 2002 was a digitally realised project across a huge number of partner schools, youth organisations, and community groups across the world. This work was happening in the context of the mainstreaming of the internet and digital technologies, alongside a broader recognition of the social and activist potential of these tools as a way of sharing information and organising around common causes. Again, C&T were keen to foreground *the process* of creating the Living Newspaper as significant, but the challenge this presented was how to facilitate an equivalent level of participant engagement to that which was created in physical workshops in a digital space. Sarah Bay Cheng has argued that participation is central to any digital performance: 'in the digital sphere, presence is defined not by physical touch but through avenues of participation. In a digitally connected and networked world, participation creates presence [...] people do not participate by "being there"; people are "there" by participating' (2010: 130). Participatory modes of theatre making are therefore suited to invoking an affect within the digital sphere as participation becomes acutely foregrounded in theatre operating on these platforms. However, the challenge remained within the project: how can the digital retain a focus on acquiring skills in critical analysis and how can emergent digital technologies be leveraged as a space of social activism?

In response to these challenges C&T developed a short animation, which established a dramaturgical frame for the young people involved in the project that sought to promote investment from the participants. This thirty-second film shifts between graphic dystopian images of surveillance cameras, satellites, war planes, herds of sheep, people in suits and anonymising masks, a hand grasping at money. Alongside these visual signifiers are a series of provocative and enigmatic statements: 'the Living Newspaper does not exist' 'to believe the news media at best ignore young people, at worst twist and distort what they SAY, DO, THINK and FEEL is self-delusion' 'the notion that young people across the world could challenge those distortions is FANTASY' 'This idea is pure theatre' (C&T, 2005). The teacher or youth leader facilitating the project on site would present this animation as something they had come across online, asking the young people for their help deciphering it. The animation introduced the form of the Living Newspaper and cast the young people as a covert network seeking to reveal truths within mediated communication. To join the project the young people had to 'hack' into the online platform (by answering a series of questions and deciphering codes) which C&T had created to share instructional films to support the making process and also enable the young people to disseminate their Living Newspapers to others in the network. The use of the instructional films (populated by three protagonists Tom, Cat, and Guy) offered the young people a series of skills and strategies for developing their own Living Newspaper, in Bay-Cheng's terms 'avenues of participation'. There was an emphasis on the importance of sharing work that did not need to be technically or aesthetically polished – with C&T – mirroring this rough DIY aesthetic in their instructional content in order to support the young people to feel able to engage regardless of their available resources, confidence with film, or training in theatre making. The use of the instructional films with Tom, Cat, and Guy cultivated the duality in the project as both work that young people could make and share in a live space together, but also performance to be disseminated to their peers as part of their contribution to a larger body of work and network of practice.

Central to the structure that C&T created were five rules that Sutton and co-writer and co-director Phil Porter – now an established playwright but at the time a member of C&T Youth Theatre – felt distilled the company's approach to Living Newspapers:

> Rule one: Be Funny
> Rule Two: Be direct
> Rule Three: Juxtapose
> Rule Four: Agitate
> Rule Five: Let the facts speak for themselves (Sutton, P, Zoom interview with authors, 28 March 2023)

Young people were encouraged to make a piece that responded to at least one of the rules. These rules acted as a distilled set of guiding principles, which enabled the work to be disseminated across a huge range of participants while also retaining a common approach and tone. Holding these rules alongside the shared editorial policy created a framework which held the process of making digitally and across distance. These rules might be seen as a descendant of Boal's principles of *teatro jornal* or the ten characteristics of the Blue Blouse, which facilitated a dissemination of a set of strategies for making theatre in accessible and politically engaged ways across South America and Russia respectively. In some instances, C&T very much held the work and the focus by curating collaborations across groups. For example, the company identified water as a thematic focus for one of the early projects and brought together young people in England, Kenya, and Australia to explore the theme from different perspectives. At this time England (Worcester in particular) was experiencing significant flooding, there were ongoing droughts in Kenya, and Australia was building multiple desalination plants. Central to C&T's project was a vision of digital Living Newspapers as a productive form for building global networks, where communities can draw on local issues but also work across commonalities to find resonances between differently located experiences. The young people therefore engaged with this given theme from their own regionally located experience but also were in dialogue with other young people about the issues around water in different global contexts. In other instances, groups signed up to the platform independently, utilising the Living Newspaper toolbox it provided to investigate the areas they were interested in and share their work on the platform. An indicative list from Sutton demonstrates the diversity of the work that emerged: high school students in Birmingham explored racial tensions in their area; MIND mental health charity utilised C&T's Living Newspaper tools to advocate for a permanent drop in centre; young women in Malawi created a sexual health education project utilising the site (Sutton, 2005: 124). Location and geography therefore remain integral to the Living Newspaper in this work, even as the digital offers new routes towards the global flow and exchange of knowledge.

In distilling the Living Newspaper down to a set of frameworks (manifesto, editorial policy, and rules) C&T developed a way in which the *process* of creating a Living Newspaper could be digitised and disseminated whilst retaining the participatory, agentic, and critical practices of the form. Sutton argues that this work

> reinvented the notion of what federated theatre activity might be, operating as a series of independent 'cells' in schools, youth theatres and communities across the globe, using digital media and websites as mechanisms for the global exchange of documentary drama materials. (Sutton, 2005: 129)

This mirrors the long-established practices of the Living Newspaper, which have always promoted wide dissemination, accessible authorship and creation, and a politically underpinned practice that promotes a critical engagement with the mediated images we encounter at a local and global scale. However, in their pioneering work imagining what a Living Newspaper might look like in a digital world, C&T's work illuminates the possibilities for this located practice in a networked world.[7]

The Royal Court and Promenade in the Pandemic

The COVID-19 pandemic threw theatre buildings across the globe into crisis. On 15 July 2020, four months into the indefinite period of theatres closures in the UK, design collective Scene Change (formed in April 2020) staged a happening which involved 110 theatres and arts organisations and over 400 freelance participants across the UK and Ireland. These participants wrapped theatre buildings across the nation in pink and white tape, reminiscent of crime scene tape, which read 'MISSING LIVE THEATRE'. This action highlighted the centrality of theatre buildings and their redundancy during the pandemic. As the collective stated, '[t]heatres which are usually teeming with life feel stark and bleak [. . .] some even shut away behind hazard tape to prevent them inadvertently being places of gathering' (Wiegand, 2020). While some theatres made use of their spaces to support public efforts to fight the pandemic, many theatre buildings were mothballed, with physical theatre spaces made redundant in a period where public gathering was variously categorised as illegal, immoral, and dangerous. Having set up the importance of site to this form and underscored the significance of mediatisation to its realisation, we now return to Walsh's reconstitutive conceptualisation of crisis, to consider how the turn to Living Newspapers allowed the Royal Court to navigate questions around what constitutes a theatre building, what is it constituted *of*, and how might its specific materiality constituted in a digital form.

[7] At the time of writing, C&T are developing a new iteration of the Living Newspaper that will draw on their Prospero platform to generate a new space for young people to engage critically and theatrically with the news.

Throughout the Royal Court's *A Counter Narrative* spectators were initially physically and then digitally transported to different spaces within the building. Consequently, the Royal Court site itself became an integral part of each performance even after it moved online. The theatre itself positioned the project as a reflection on 'the strange and contradictory relationship between a closed theatre building and the world outside' (Royal Court Theatre, 2021b). When *A Counter Narrative* was launched in Autumn 2020 it was initially intended to be a building-based project that took the form of a socially distanced site-specific performance, which would be recorded and available for audiences to watch online. The theatre's press release announced '[i]t will be performed in promenade, taking audiences, in person and online, around the Royal Court building on a journey never before available to the public in this way' (Royal Court, 2020d). Masked audiences would be guided around the theatre in small groups to witness different vignettes of performance around the building. The materiality of the building, and the specific categorisation of the spaces, becomes a kind of co-author of the work. As *Arts Desk* reviewer Laura De Lisle noted 'this is, ultimately, a love letter to the Royal Court, with its nooks and crannies and stages and substages filled with bric-a-brac from long-ago shows' (2020). In presenting the various spaces and the traces they contain, each of the performance sites operate as a kind of palimpsest for what it is to be in a theatre and invite a kind of yearning for a return to the building (and all that such a return would mean), which is threaded through the project. As t' Hart asserts, 'crises provide opportunities for mass mobilisation and institutional self-dramatisation', the Royal Court's *A Counter Narrative* sought to engage a mass audience, in part, through unfolding a narrative of the theatre building (1993: 40). Further, in opening out seemingly the whole building (although the office spaces remained unused) the project invoked a feeling of transparency and ownership of the theatre as a collective cultural resource. As journalist Arifa Akbar reflects after seeing Edition One,

> in the end, the show is not just about the inner workings of a newspaper but about the inside of a theatre and its accessibility. It demystifies the usually hallowed spaces in a theatre, presenting all of itself to us, from the backstage oil of the engine room to front-of-stage glory. It seems to say that this is not for the privileged few. It belongs to us. (2020)

In part through opening up the building in this way, the Royal Court replicated the experience of a kind of public art and collective creation that the Living Newspaper has historically invoked (from Federal Theatre Project to *Teatro Jornal*). Even though the work did not happen in public spaces or with specific communities, it explicitly sought to bring new publics into different spaces in the building in order to affirm the importance of the theatre as site. This is not the first time the Royal Court has opened up its multiple spaces to the public. When current Artistic Director Vicky Featherstone took the reins she programmed Open Court, trailed with the tagline 'the writers have the keys' to the building', this six week festival involved 140 writers ideas and staged 40 new plays in different spaces within the building. The Royal Court then, has its own history of demystifying the theatre building; however, we argue that in the context of a period of theatre closures *A Counter Narrative* went beyond a sharing of 'hallowed spaces', and offered a homage to the materiality of theatre sites which had been left dark for so long. Indeed, across the timespan of the project (December 2020–April 2021), there is an ongoing rumination on what it is to assemble in performance spaces; from the tentative return apparent in the socially distanced promenade of Edition One to Messias' embodiment of the building calling audiences back in Edition Six, *A Counter Narrative* tracks and contributes to a discourse around theatre sites in the COVID-19 pandemic.

However, the project is not singularly one of nostalgia, while it continually reflects on what it might mean to return, to go back, it also considers where we might instead choose to go forward, to go elsewhere. This idea is a persistent refrain in the content of the performances but also in the spatial configuration of the theatre itself. As Joanne Tompkins argues in her work on the politics of theatre spaces the 'enactment of space in performance has the capacity to demonstrate the rethinking and reordering of space, power, and knowledge by locating worldmaking spaces and places tangibly, albeit transiently' (2014: 6). Performance can temporarily challenge the ways in which space is categorised in the ways it addresses and intervenes in spatial relations. *A Counter Narrative* temporarily reoriented the very building it occupied. With performances being staged in the auditorium downstairs, the upstairs studio space, the substage, the scene dock, the library, the foyer, the lift, and the tech box. The use of the theatre building then was framed as a further innovation of the Living Newspaper form, here occupying multiple spaces across one theatre building. Each space within the building offered a set of parameters for playwrights to produce work within: the substage became a club space for marginalised and LGBTQ+ stories; the technical box was framed as 'The Control Room', a space to explore our relationships with technology; the bar was presented as a dating space; the green room was given over to an ongoing Weather Installation; the Agony Aunt section was located in the Cloak room; the Horoscopes occupied the women's toilets; the Obituaries occurred in the theatre's back staircase and lift. Other spaces in the building were contextualised as more flexible with the Jerwood Studio Upstairs being framed as a white box space, a blank canvas; the bookshop as an evolving shifting space; and the box office operated as a news stand, for shorter stories. The attachment of given themes to specific locations across the project speaks to the ways in which space is imbued with particular social and cultural realities. Some relationships are quite literal (green room and weather, technologies and technical box); while others knowingly invoke, and potentially reinforce, a spatial politics around gender and identity – LGBTQ work in the basement, horoscopes as feminised. The creative collectives involved in *A Counter Narrative* regularly play up against and with the politics of the spatial frameworks constructed by the theatre.

It is important to note that the works produced regularly break out of these spatial structures. For example, we opened this section with a queer performance that happened on the front steps of the theatre. Similarly, queer theatre maker Travis Alabanza's work was presented in the box office (rather than the substage); yet it did still explicitly address the spatial politics of the Royal Court and theatrical institutions more broadly. In *An Ode to the Underground and Ms Sharon Le Grand* (Edition Three), drag queen and performance artist Ms Sharon Le Grand muses on the invitation inside the Royal Court:

> I had no idea you were all up here, above ground, courting around and choosing which monologue to recite next! I had no bloody idea you were mid zoom plays, and petitions and emergency grant schemes [. . .]
>
> Because I was in my tiny little no-art-just-arson hole, below the fucking ground, where I've been for all these bloody years – where there must not be a culture to recover? No artiste to save? No theatre box office to rally behind?
>
> [. . .]
>
> You see, in my tiny little hole, well – it isn't actually that tiny – it is in fact a gaping, large, expanding, inclusive, wide, all encompassing, underground, dark but beautiful, gaping – did I say gaping? – hole? That is filled with monsters and queers and fuck jobs and pervs and politics and party and artists and geniuses and fucking comedians and trailblazers and people that did not even know that this 'party' above ground was bloody happening . . .
>
> Or maybe we just are used to not being invited? (Alabanza, 2021)

Some works invoked the spatial politics of the building to speak to a wider knowledge of the economic, cultural, and political power dynamics at play in the theatre sector, which were acutely affirmed during the crisis of the pandemic. Here Alabanza engages with the Royal Court building in the content of their piece in order to challenge the dominant structures and rhetoric that pervades the sector. However, in the decision to site the work in 'hidden' spaces around the venue there is at least a symbolic decentring of the mainstage – barring one use of it in Rory Mullarkey's *This Play* (Edition Six) – the stage in the main auditorium is never used. The Front Page for each edition occurs in the main house but performers occupy the auditorium facing spectators on the stage. This deprivileging of the main space signifies a broader commitment across the project to prioritise narratives that are often marginalised in the UK theatre sector. The crisis then specifically shapes the spatial dramaturgies of the project in the way sites within theatre buildings are recategorised and in the wider political logic of the project to create spaces for (some) marginalised voices to speak back to the world through the form of the Living Newspaper in this moment of upheaval.

As well as enabling multiple performances to occur at the same time, this spacing around the building also served to make the event safer as audiences were dispersed and socially distanced. The press release announcing the project explained: 'Performances will take place throughout the day from 11am – 11pm [. . .]. Enhanced safety measures will be in place throughout the building to support a socially distant audience'. (Royal Court Theatre, 2020c). The audience travel through the theatre and its different spaces, in small, staggered, and socially distanced groups. In this brief period between lockdowns in the UK, theatres tentatively opened their doors and tried to find new ways through which to hold audiences safely in live performance. The project wrestled with the idea of what it might mean to be a theatre building in a world in which audiences could not collectively gather. In this new world, the architecture of European theatre buildings was therefore constituted as insufficient for facilitating performance and spectatorship. Projects like *A Counter Narrative* were required to shift the ways in which such spaces were used and navigated by creatives and audiences in order to render them usable.

As well as taking place in person in promenade, Edition One could also be viewed online. There was a concerted effort to replicate or refract the experience of going to the theatre building in this edition. Notably, across the streamed version, interspersed intermittently between the different performances were moments where the digital spectators would move through some of the theatre's spaces as if navigating the building as a visitor and 'encounter' a member of the Front of House staff in a corridor, on a stairwell, or in the foyer. The moving through the corridors and stairwells between spaces felt like an attempt not necessarily to replicate but to refract the material experience of being in a theatre building, to illuminate the gap between occupying the space and witnessing it through a screen. Each of these encounters were no more than a minute and with a different masked staff member who would, reading from a script, speak directly to camera.

> 'I hope we're all doing ok. We should ask ourselves that. Let's ask ourselves are we ok?'
>
> 'We should pause here [. . .] Think about how vulnerable that trust makes us but at the same time how necessary it is'
>
> 'The invisible people that become visible and the ones we thought were vital that were no use at all'

As well as offering a refracted experience of being *in* the theatre itself, these moments of encounter foreground the often-unacknowledged labour of front of house staff and highlight the heightened anxieties about a return to collective gathering. There is a recognition of the care these staff offer in supporting audiences as they return to the building. More broadly, these interjections invite a wider reflection on the myriad of undervalued and underpaid key workers (people working in care, transport, food production, and retail sectors) whose labour was only recognised as vital in the face of a global health crisis.

As Edition Two was being developed the UK experienced a second wave of COVID and at a time when different regions of the country were put into localised lockdowns. The Royal Court made the decision to move this edition entirely online. Then, at the start of 2021, the UK went into a full national lockdown and the Royal Court paused the project in order to find a way to produce it effectively under the restricted conditions. The theatre then engaged TEA Films, a London-based production company who regularly film theatrical production, to support the delivery of the project as a series of filmed and digitally disseminated performance. At the start of March 2021, the Royal Court issued a press release outlining the new shape of the project:

> The Living Newspaper experience has been re-imagined for the upcoming four editions exclusively for an online audience at home. Each weekly online edition will now be delivered to ticket holders over five days – with new content shared daily including local and global perspectives [. . .]. Every edition will launch with a live streamed performance of The Front Page at the beginning of the week. Audience numbers for the live stream will be limited due to the nature of the collective experience where viewers can see each other on screen. (Royal Court, 2020)

This digital iteration of *A Counter Narrative* therefore more closely mirrored the rolling news cycle of the contemporary media landscape, with works responding to the news of the moment landing in audience inboxes daily. The Front Page remained as a kind of collective gathering point, but one in a digital space, for audiences to share spectatorship with one another through a digital platform that allowed you to see other audience members. However, this was a singular experience in each edition, with the other 'clippings' as they were termed being sent directly to ticketholders to view in their own time. This restructuring of the project due to the shifting COVID restrictions therefore pushed the Royal Court to more resonantly replicate the contemporary media landscape this project intervened in. The move to online spaces as a site of dissemination for the Living Newspaper brought into sharp focus the increasingly digital circulation of news and prompted a consideration of what such media consumption means for contemporary iterations of the Living Newspaper.

Conclusion

> We're trying to make theatre and how do you encode the theatricality? Creating theatricality digitally rather than going, we're making something for the web.
> (Sutton, P, Zoom interview with authors, 28 March 2023)

The Living Newspaper is a powerful example of the generative potential of crisis. A form which has continually evolved within and been shaped by – in its structure, dissemination, and content – successive crises. Foregrounding the significance and interconnectedness of site, materiality, and mediation has enabled us to interrogate how three distinct examples of Living Newspapers navigate the live and mediated performance. Space and mediatisation have been central to the practice of the form across its history; they have been shaped by its ideological underpinnings of public accessibility and political mobilisation, they have informed its aesthetics and generated its content. Living Newspapers demonstrate the networked and overlapping – rather than binary – relationship between the material and the mediated. The Blue Blouses, C&T, and the Royal Court demonstrate the layered mediatisation of the form across different technological ages and affirm the ways in which the form remains attentive to, and affected by, its site in production. The relationship between site and media comes into particularly sharp focus in *A Counter Narrative*, a distinct offer during a period in which theatre buildings were shut down. Rather than a shift to a digital only offering, the Royal Court engaged with the Living Newspaper as a way to invite audiences into their building and assert the power of theatre sites even when spectators themselves could not be present in them. Material space remains a potent political and artistic signifier even in the digital sphere and in a moment of crisis in which we, as audiences, could not occupy it.

4 Crisis Time(s), Temporality, and the Living Newspaper

Time is a fundamental structure of news, performance, and crisis. The timeliness of the Living Newspaper to engage with a crisis as it unfolds and be reactive to changing conditions demarcates it as a responsive form. Although many Living Newspapers were pre-scripted in the early Russian experiments with the form, due to the ever-shifting news cycle, the troupes of players who toured Russia during the Civil War sometimes only established the form of each sketch prior to going on stage. As Robert Leach recounts, 'On one occasion an agitator interrupted the performance to announce the defeat of [Russian General in the White Army Anton Ivanovich] Denikin. The audience burst out cheering and the actors improvised a scene of Denikin dancing, then being chased off by Red Army soldiers' (Leach, 1994: 87). Similarly, Britain's Unity Theatre's Living Newspaper *Crisis a.k.a Czechoslovakia* was written 72 hours prior to its opening night, scheduled to coincide with British Prime Minister Neville Chamberlain's meeting with Hitler in Munich in 1938. There is therefore an immediacy that contributes to some of the sense of *liveness* in the Living Newspaper. Concurrently, several of the examples explored across these pages were longer form investigations of contemporary concerns; for example, many of the Federal Theatre Project Living Newspapers consisted of plays that were researched and created over a period of months and then staged across a long run, using the same material on loop and creating a repository of scripts that could be reused and repeated across decades. Time, though, remains acutely important to these longer form Living Newspapers, which move beyond responsivity and instead stand as a slower engagement with the complexities of crisis and act as an archive of the moment they emerged from.

A turn to crisis management scholarship and practices reveals this field is also acutely concerned with considerations of time. Indeed, crisis is so deeply predicated on a rupture of before and after; it is shaped by 'the deep uncertainty that comes with a forced departure from the known past to one of the many possible alternative futures' (Rosenthal, Boin, and Comfort, 2001: 20). Consequently, crisis is therefore both bound up with the moment of shift from past to possible futures. An attention to crisis management underlines how we can productively hold both the immediate and the long term together:

> Crisis managers vacillate between immediate action and long-term effectiveness. Traditional crisis management repertoires are marked by a preoccupations with the 'here and now' of the situation: the acute threat must be dealt with. [. . .]. The modern crisis, however, is a long-term process rather than an event. Long after the onset of the crisis has occurred, crisis managers are confronted with problems that may take on the form of the 'crisis after the crisis'. (Rosenthal, Boin, and Comfort, 2001: 19)

Crisis management scholarship illuminates the plurality of crisis time, there is a splitting of attention between the urgent and immediate on the one hand and the future and the enduring on the other. Time not only becomes a central focus, but also remains in tension, holding together the present and the possible futures which will continue to require critical decision making. As Boin, Rosenthal, Comfort assert, contemporary crises must engage with the cycles and perpetuations of ongoing and intersecting crises, rather than only deciding on the immediate action (2001). This affirms the centrality of time to any study of crisis and also highlights the need to recognise its different permutations, rather than accepting a linear model of crisis events and resolutions. Across this Element, we have illuminated the contingent structures of the Living Newspaper, from rapid response agitprop style commentaries on the news of the day (Boal, C&T, and Blue Blouses) to longer investigative work of capturing and engaging with enduring political concerns in a given context (*Born in the RSA* and the Federal Theatre Project). We now turn to consider how different temporalities of crisis are made manifest in the performance and production practices of the Royal Court's *A Counter Narrative*.

Alongside attending to the different modalities of crisis time, we explore the particular affect of crisis in theatre. Living Newspapers have a specific relationship to theatre makers and spectators' *experiences* of time. As Geographer Susan Mayhew has noted

> in contrast to the measurable and calculated notion of time/chronology, temporality is concerned with the way in which a sequence of events, a kind of history, is physically experienced by those who live through them or experience them. Thus, the passing of time is treated not as a neutral dimension but rather as being constituted by social practices. (Mayhew, 2015: 486)

Beyond chronological frameworks of time, in this section we also attend to the temporalities of the Living Newspaper and how this is shaped by lived experiences of crisis. Both of them reference the ways in which theatre makers and spectators experience the specific processes of the Living Newspaper and asserts the ways in which the affective capacity of performance offers new perspectives on how we can experience and depict the distinctive and multiple temporalities of crisis. We will illuminate how Living Newspapers, then, in their capturing of multiple temporalities, can be understood to produce an embodied time-capsule of a crisis.

Temporalities of Crisis: Fast and Creeping

Crisis management researchers have identified two temporalities of crisis, 'fast' and 'slow' burning and the COVID-19 pandemic has been variously defined as both ('t Hart & Boin, 2001). Fast-burning crises are discrete disruptive events with clear parameters that emerge seemingly from nowhere and require a time-pressured urgent response while the situation is still being deciphered. In this sense, the pandemic was fast burn, requiring immediate health responses, causing unparalleled disruption to global financial markets, and demanding significant communal action while understandings were still developing.

As Section 1 outlines the Royal Court's programming of seven Living Newspapers was in response to the suspension of the theatre sector. Alongside this immediate materialist response, Artistic Director Vicky Featherstone also outlined the need for the theatre return with 'something which would embrace the spirit of what we were learning over this time. It could be political, it could be fast, it could be responsive' (Hemming, 2020). Featherstone's desire to capture the speed with which the theatre sector was reacting and reorienting itself in the context of the COVID-19 pandemic echoes the temporality of the fast burning crisis. Lucy Morrison has articulated how 'the idea was to move at a fairly high pace as a collective so that [there was] the opportunity for writers to absorb the news that was happening in the week of / week before the edition' and as such edition collectives 'started meetings no more than 6 weeks before the edition was due' (Morrison, L, Email to authors, 20 March 2023.).[8] The process of engaging the theatre makers involved and facilitating the writers to begin the commission was both enforced by the context of COVID-19 – which mirror time-pressured critical decision making that is required in the fast burn crisis model – and also partially shaped by the theatre and the form of Living Newspaper itself. There was an intention in requiring the collectives to begin meetings no earlier than six weeks in advance – this structuring of the timeline of the project required artists to make responsive work that was bound up with the immediate moment surrounding their edition.

Yet, as COVID-19 unfolded, the temporalities operating within it also developed. Slow burn, or what Boin, Ekengren, and Rhinard term 'creeping crises' have 'a long incubation time and may keep simmering long after the 'hot phase' of the crisis is over. It does not have a clear beginning or ending. It can remain undefined for a long time' (2020: 119). The temporalities at play in *A Counter Narrative* mirrored this melding of fast and slow burn as performances unfolded to reveal a set of intersecting and ongoing creeping crises that accompanied the COVID-19 pandemic. Two of the most pertinent examples of this can be seen in Front Page *Crisis after Crisis, We Persist* and durational installation 'The Weather Room'.

Appearing as 'The Front Page', a segment always collectively written by the playwrights working on the newspaper that week and performed amongst the seating bank of the main theatre, *Crisis after Crisis, We Persist* opened Edition Four. The content of the piece focused on the endurance of collective action. Five actors occupy the auditorium, they are all people of colour, each has a mic stand in front of them and holds a household item (a metal sieve, a pan, a glass bottle) that is repurposed into a percussive instrument. The piece is initially underscored by a disjointed, offbeat and fragmented soundscape, with performers interjecting with singular words or phrases of call and response including 'Persist', 'Protest' 'PROTEST Persists'. As a rhythm starts to emerge the performance bursts to life and draws directly from a Black Lives Matter protest chant,

[8] It is of note that even this pace was not stable as recurring lockdowns resulted in production timeline variations for several editions. Morrison, L. (2023) Unpublished correspondence with Sarah Bartley and Sarah Mullan over email.

1+2: Back up back up we want freedom freedom
All your racist sexist cops we don't need em need em
(Black Tam et al., 2021)

The invocation of the Black Lives Matter movement demands a fresh attention to the ongoing crisis of state and systemic violence encountered by Black people in the UK and internationally. This refrain also calls attention to the immediate context of Edition Four, which was produced in April 2021, as Kill The Bill rallies swept the UK in response to the government's Police and Crime Sentencing Bill, which sought to restrict the right to assemble and criminalise 'noisy' or disruptive forms of protest; introduce new trespass laws targeting Gypsy, Roma and Traveller people; and expand police stop and search powers, which already disproportionately impact Black people. In the second verse, the focus then shifts to 2021 protests around gender-based violence in Lima, Peru and the broader South American feminist movement.

Alerta, alerta, alerta que camina
Mujeres feminista por las calles de Lima (Black Tam et al., 2021)

This transboundary exploration of crisis is carried through by a turn to attend to the refugee crisis. The stage directions ask the performers to call 'All Out of Sync' the phrase: 'NO HUMAN IS ILLEGAL' (Black Tam et al., 2021). This 'out of synch-ness' threads throughout the ten-minute performance with the echoes of statements jarring and overlapping one another evoking a sense of multiple, intersecting, states of chaos, competing for attention, without a defined start or end point. *Crisis after Crisis, We Persist* is indicative of the attention to 'creeping crises' that the Living Newspaper, in its expanded temporalities, responsivity, sheer mass of material, and multiplicity of perspectives allows for.

A complex temporality is then further embedded within *A Counter Narrative* through the weather room 'an installation designed to evoke changing weather states. A space to contemplate our own impact on the climate crisis' that appears in every edition. A large glass box of sand looms in the centre of the Royal Court's Green Room in Chris Thorpe's *Weather Room – extract from Always Maybe The Last Time*. Appearing in Edition One, Thorpe's play was initially programmed as part of OPEN COURT: CLIMATE EMERGENCY, 'a series of performances, lectures, and workshops to help us prepare psychologically, collectively and practically for a transformed future'. Cancelled due to the first COVID-19 lockdown in March 2020, the recurring weather room feature can be read as a reworking of the Open Court focus, positioning climate change as an issue requiring responsivity even as the world is reckoning with an unfolding pandemic (Royal Court, 2020).

As the only feature across the Royal Court project with thematically specific content, the recurrence of The Weather Room demands that attention continues to be paid to a slow-burn crisis and asks for the multiplicity of intersecting crises to be continually witnessed across the edition. This is particularly pertinent given that protection responses to COVID-19 such as using PPE increased the demand for single use plastics and subsequently plastic waste has surged (Benson et al., 2021). Across Editions One to Three, the glass box's internal environment develops: the sand that is initially empty becomes littered with objects; a sunlounger, a bucket, baby bottles as Ruby Thomas's *Romy and Me* recounts getting arrested at a climate protest as an act for a future niece and Anupama Chandrasekhar's *Where Things Go To Die* invites us to look at a series of treasures (children's toothbrushes, plastic bag, a condom) that have been preserved for a hundred years by a sea-dwelling population. The lack of embodied presence in these initial editions underscoring the threat of a future without humans. In Editions Five and Six onwards, performers appear within the box but at various moments the action is obscured as smoke billows in, water runs down the walls, and films of dirt and condensation that have developed as a result of the box's internal climate.

Ruptured Temporalities

Fast burn and creeping are articulations of the ways in which crises unfold and sit within a linear temporal framework of forward progression. However, As Limor Samimian-Darash and Nir Rotem assert, crisis 'marks a break in the usual flow of experience [. . .] a break in history' (Samimian-Darash and Rotem, 2019: 921). The affect of a rupture in time, suspended rather than flowing as normal, was acutely felt during COVID-19 where frameworks of time under capitalism were initially disrupted through furlough schemes, working from home, and the closure of many retail industries and leisure activities. The threat the pandemic brought foreclosed the future, activities that structured time in the present were (for large sections of the global population) dissolved, and the past now felt like a disjuncture from the 'new normal'.

In *A Counter Narrative* theatre makers used this experience of *suspended* time to interrogate temporalities as disrupted, in flux, unending, collapsing, delayed, stuck, repeated, disconnected, cyclical, and colliding. In Caro Black Tam's *Short Term Memory*, a person walks down the internal staircase of the theatre sticking protest posters to the walls without glue. The posters immediately fall off. Once the person reaches the bottom of the staircase, they take the lift back to the top, and begin the process again. Tanika Gupta's *Mirror on the Moor* tracks UK Chancellor Rishi Sunak and Home Secretary Priti Patel's clandestine attempt to discover who will be the first Asian Prime Minister through the procurement of a magic mirror. Staged as a Bollywood Soap with melodramatic music, sound effects and close face to camera shots, the piece calls on the past to reveal the present. The know-it-all mirror is revealed to contain former Conservative Prime Minister Margaret Thatcher. Many of Thatcher's responses are transposed verbatim from a 1978 Granada TV interview in which she criticised the immigration of Black and Global Majority people after which her popularity increased and she was subsequently elected PM. The piece illuminates how disconnected from the past of the Conservative party Sunak and Patel are as they squabble and seek to demonstrate to Thatcher how they uphold and embody Conservative party values including anti-immigration. Thatcher leaves asserting 'over my cold dead body' will there be a Black or Brown leader of the Conservative party and as Sunak attempts to resummon her Dadabhai Naoroji the first Indian MP elected in the UK (in 1891) who neither are familiar with appears. Naoroji compels Sunak (ultra-elite imperialist) and Patel (lacking humanity) to consider their history before deeming both unfit to serve as PM. *Mirror on the Moor* engages thematically with this experience of disrupted temporalities to reflect on a broader dislocation of politicians from history occurring in the contemporary UK. Ironically, two years later in 2023 Rishi Sunak did become the UK Prime Minister after losing the Conservative Party Leadership Election to Liz Truss who's catastrophic forty-nine-day premiership resulted in her resignation and Sunak leading the country. This suspended time has become unstuck then, for the Sunak of *Mirror on the Moor*.

Conclusion

A Counter Narrative is propelled and shaped by the unfolding fast and creeping crisis of COVID-19, concurrently as a project it occupies a break in time and utilises this as an opportunity to explore the potential of other seemingly out of reach temporalities, bringing these alternative configurations of time into view in this suspended perpetual present. In this way, *A Counter Narrative* illuminates how we use time to make sense of the world and offers a provocation to consider how we might utilise the experience of *suspended time* to understand a specific moment of crisis. Janet Roitman's understanding of crisis as 'a history of the present' asserts that the act of naming an event as a crisis, reveals the priorities of the present, and establishes a moment as historically significant (Roitman, 2014). *A Counter Narrative* experiments with multiple approaches to undertaking histories of the present during a period of suspended time. The cumulative impact of a multiplicity of experiments with time, that mine trans-historical and transnational temporalities, across all seven editions of the project, offer different formations in order to interrogate how we might make sense of our present.

Conclusion: The Living Newspaper as Crisis Theatre

> ACTOR 3: This play is about how I always used to want plays about the world, but I've had enough of the world now. I've had enough of sad chaos, and everyday death. I've tried to grind on through this long and slow emergency with as much kindness and gentleness and grace as I can but just . . .
> Give me plays again now, just . . .
> Give me bums and harlequins. And just stuff my eyes with cunning servants and I'll cherish it, I swear.
> ACTOR 1: This play is about someone who loves something.
> ACTOR 3: This play is about some people lost in a very dark wood.
> ACTOR 1: This play is about the plays that didn't happen. That couldn't happen. That won't happen
> ACTOR 2: This play is about the plays that will happen.
> ACTOR 1: This play is about to be over, but it isn't over yet.
> (Mullarkey, 2021)

This Play by Rory Mullarkey was the only performance to happen on the Royal Court mainstage across all seven editions of *A Counter Narrative*. Performers Louise Harland, Sule Rimi, and Millicent Wong move from the auditorium seats to the stage as they roll through a multitude of imagined, half-remembered, or misinterpreted plays. With the recurrent refrain 'This play is . . . 'they cycle through narrative mazes of the powerful and the powerless, of fraught and funny relationships, of metaphors and tangible realities. The piece weaves a range of intersecting and distinct plots, folktales, and characters, familiar and unfamiliar, into one another. It also meditates on the ways audiences experience plays ('this play is about three hours long not including two intervals, which I didn't realise until interval two meant actually more like three hours forty. And now I've missed my train home') or critics review them, reeling through increasingly absurd rationales for different star ratings. But beyond stories, audiences, critics, and the act of making theatre, *This Play* is about *those* plays, the ones that never happened because of COVID-19. It is about imagining them all, out loud, on the Royal Court Theatre stage. And also imagining that they might still happen, which is – in May 2021 (and even still at the time of writing in 2023) – an act of hope. *This Play* mirrors the broader project of *A Counter Narrative* in the ways it documents, mourns, speaks back to, and finds ways to both imagine in a period of crisis and conceive the world beyond this crisis.

Shradha Kundra and Rohit Dwivedi argue that crises 'shatter fundamental assumptions and trigger sensemaking about the event, the self, and often the world at large'(2023: 131). The Living Newspaper offers frameworks through which to undertake sensemaking *during* the crisis event: Boal's 11 principles, Simon's montage, Federal Theatre Project's themes, Blue Blouse 10 characteristics, C&T's 5 rules, Royal Court's content frames are all strategies to develop understandings of our world. The form sits alongside and within crisis, trying to make sense of events as they are unfolding and evolving. As Matthew Seeger and Timothy Sellnow have asserted the 'meaning deficit of a crisis creates a discursive space that is filled by narratives, often multiple and conflicting' (2016: 7). Creating performance in a context of confusion and ambiguity, produces a particular dramaturgy. As we have shown in the case studies explored here, the Living Newspaper regularly resists a singular sequential narrative that seeks to affirm a monolithic experience of an event; rather, this form consistently embraces the abundance of narratives that emerge in a crisis and stages this multiplicity. As Christophe Roux-Dufort argues, in a crisis 'it is not so much the loss of meaning that overwhelms [. . .] but rather the wave of meaning that cannot be processed through the traditional frameworks of interpretation' (Roux-Dufort, 2007: 111). For him, crises produce an 'overflow of meaning' which we argue the Living Newspaper is capable of capturing in its material, spatial, and temporal practices. In this way, it constitutes crisis theatre because its dramaturgy is imbued with the *affect* of a crisis event – the experience of an overflow of meaning – rather than the construction of 'tidier' narratives that occur in the aftermath.

In this Element we have investigated the Living Newspaper – across different moments in time and in different geographical locations – through a prism of crisis in order to illuminate the ways in which this form has persistently appeared in, and indeed been forged by, periods of crisis. Living Newspapers have been absent from existing performance scholarship engaging with crisis; in attending to this absence we assert the utility of examining the strategies of this form as a way to develop a deeper understanding of the material, affective, spatial, and temporal potential of theatre practices in periods of crisis. While the political, social, and economic nature of the contexts covered in these pages differs (Russian Civil War, USA in the Great Depression, the military dictatorship in Brazil, apartheid in South Africa, media censorship and misrepresentation of marginalised subjects, the COVID-19 pandemic), the reoccurrence of the Living Newspaper in moments of rupture, emergency, turmoil or reorientation is significant.

By holding this diverse collection of examples together, we assert the Living Newspaper as a crisis theatre. That is performance borne out of crisis and formulated by it, taking on the very qualities of the crisis it is enmeshed in. Beyond simply staging or responding to crisis, such theatre is imbued with crisis in the production, content, and consumption of performance. Living Newspaper is one form of crisis theatre, investigating it here has delineated a set of qualities that belong to crisis theatre; we advocate for a wider application of this term to capture and categorise the material particularities and creative strategies of theatres borne out of and imbued with crisis.

References

Adams D. and Goldbard, A. (1985) 'New Deal Cultural Programs: Experiments in Cultural Democracy', *WWCD*, www.wwcd.org/policy/US/newdeal.html#FTNT_6.

Adams, C. (2021) 'News on Stage: Towards Re-configuring Journalism through Theatre to a Public Sphere', *Journalism Practice* 15(8), 1163–1180.

Akbar, A. (2020) 'The Royal Court Becomes a Living Newspaper Complete with Musical Headlines', *Guardian*, 11 December. www.theguardian.com/stage/2020/dec/11/the-royal-court-becomes-a-living-newspaper-complete-with-musical-headlines.

Alabanza, T. (2021) 'An Ode to the Underground and Ms Sharon Le Grand', in *A Counternarrative: Edition Three*. London: The Royal Court Theatre.

Angelaki, V. (2017) *Social and Political Theatre in 21st-Century Britain: Staging Crisis*. London: Bloomsbury.

Arent, A (1968) 'Ethiopia': The First 'Living Newspaper', *Educational Theatre Journal* 20(1), 15–31.

Babbage, F. (2004) *Augusto Boal*. London: Routledge.

Banks M. and O'Connor, J. (2021) '"A Plague upon Your Howling": Art and Culture in the Viral Emergency', *Cultural Trends* 30(1), 3–18.

Bay-Cheng, S. (2010) 'Theatre History and Digital Historiography', in *Theater Historiography: Critical Interventions*, H. Bial and S. Magelssen eds., Ann Arbor: University of Michigan Press, 125–36.

Benson, N. U., Bassey, D. E., and Palanisami, T. (2021) COVID Pollution: Impact of COVID-19 Pandemic on Global Plastic Waste Footprint, *Heliyon* 7, 2.

Black Tam, C., Gregg, S., Gupta,T. et al. (2021) 'Crisis after Crisis We Persist', in *A Counternarrative: Edition 4*. London: Royal Court Theatre.

Boal, A. (1998) *Legislative Theatre: Using Performance to Make Politics*, trans. by Adrian Jackson. London: Routledge.

Boin, A., Ekengren, M., and Rhinard, M. (2020) 'Hiding in Plain Sight: Conceptualizing the Creeping Crisis', *Risks, Hazards & Crisis in Public Policy* 11, 116–138, 121.

Bradby, D., and McCormick, J. (1978) *Peoples Theatre*. Maryland: Croom Helm Rowman And Littlefield

C&T (2005) 'Living Newspaper Manifesto', *YouTube*, https://www.youtube.com/watch?v=bH1VzIGCzlA.

Butler, L. (2021) 'Obituary', in *A Counter Narrative: Edition 3*. London: Royal Court Theatre,

Casson, J. W. (2000) 'Living Newspaper: Theatre and Therapy'. *TDR*, 44(2), 107–122

Chambers, C. (1989) *The Story of Unity Theatre*. United Kingdom: Lawrence and Wishart.

Committee of Public Accounts (2021) 'Covid 19: Culture Recovery Fund', 14 June, House of Commons Library. https://committees.parliament.uk/work/1136/covid19-culture-recovery-fund/publications/.

Cosgrove, S. (1982) The Living Newspaper: History, Production and Form. Thesis, University of Hull.

Davies, L. (2020) 'Written Evidence Submitted by the Royal Court Theatre', Call for Evidence Impact of Covid-19 on DCMS sectors, UK Parliament, 16 April. https://committees.parliament.uk/writtenevidence/1733/html/.

De Lisle, L. (2020) 'Living Newspaper: A Counter Narrative, Royal Court Online Review –The News, but Better', 24 December, *The Arts Desk*. https://theartsdesk.com/theatre/living-newspaper-counter-narrative-royal-court-online-review-%E2%80%93-news-better.

Delgado, M., and Svich, C. (2002) *Theatre in Crisis? Performance Manifestos for a New Century*. United Kingdom: Manchester University Press.

Dowden, O. (6 July 2020) Interviewed on BBC Breakfast.

Drain, R. (2002) *Twentieth Century Theatre: A Sourcebook*. United Kingdom: Taylor & Francis.

Edmondson, G., and Mladek, K. (eds.) (2017) *Sovereignty in Ruins: A Politics of Crisis*. Durham: Duke University Press.

Flanagan, H. (1935) *Instructions – Federal Theatre Projects*, Works Progress Administration October 1935, retrieved from the Library of Congress. www.loc.gov/item/farbf.00010002/.

Flanagan, H. (1969) *Arena: The History of the Federal Theatre*. Washington, DC: Limelight Editions.

Florisson, R., O'Brien, D., Taylor, M., McAndrew, S., and Feder, T. (2021) 'The Impact of Covid-19 on Jobs in the Cultural Sector –Part 3', *culturehive.co.uk*. www.culturehive.co.uk/CVIresources/the-impact-of-covid-19-on-jobs-in-the-cultural-sector-part-3/.

Forsythe, A. and Megson, C. (eds.) (2009) *Get Real: Documentary Theatre Past and Present*. United Kingdom: Palgrave Macmillan.

Fraden, R. (1996) *Blueprints for a Black Federal Theatre*. United Kingdom: Cambridge University Press.

Francis-Devine, B., Powell, A., and Clark, H. (2022) 'Coronavirus: Impact on the Labour Market', *House of Commons Library*, 9 August. https://commonslibrary.parliament.uk/research-briefings/cbp-8898/#:~:text=The%20number%20of%20people%20in,to%20the%20lowest%20since%201994.

Franklin D Rooservelt Library. (n.d.) 'Great Depression Facts', *Franklin D Rooservelt Library*, www.fdrlibrary.org/great-depression-facts.

Gamson, W. A., Croteau, D., Hoynes, W., and Sasson T. (1992) 'Media Images and the Social Construction of Reality', *Annual Review of Sociology* 18, 373–93.

Ginwala, F. (1973) 'The Press in South Africa', *Index on Censorship* 2(3), 27–43.

Gray, A. (1990) 'Born at The Market', in *A Contemporary Theatre: Born in the RSA Programme*. Seattle: Encore Publishing.

Hemming, S. (2020) 'Sarah Hemming Writing on Living Newspaper in the Financial Times', Royal Court Theatre, December 20. https://royalcourttheatre.com/sarah-hemming-writing-on-living-newspaper-in-the-financial-times/.

Henley, D. (2022) 'Time for Change: Working Freelance in Creativity and Culture', *artscouncil.org.uk*, 11 April. www.artscouncil.org.uk/blog/time-change-working-freelance-creativity-and-culture.

Hutchinson, Y. (2009) 'Verbatim Theatre in South Africa: "Living History in a Person's Performance"', in *Get Real: Documentary Theatre Past and Present*, A. Forsyth, and C. Megson, eds., United Kingdom: Palgrave Macmillan, 209–223.

Hutchison, Y. (2003) 'Barney Simon: Brokering Cultural Interventions', *Contemporary Theatre Review* 13(3), 4–15.

Jeffers, A. (2011) *Refugees, Theatre and Crisis: Performing Global Identities*. United Kingdom: Palgrave Macmillan.

Kondo, D. (2018) *Worldmaking: Race, Performance, and the Work of Creativity*. Durham: Duke University Press.

Kundra, S. and Dwivedi, R. (2023) Sensemaking of COVIDian Crisis for Work and Organization, *Philosophy of Management* 22(1), 129–47.

Kruger, L. (1992) *The National Stage: Theatre and Cultural Legitimation in England, France, and America*. Chicago: University of Chicago Press.

Leach, R. (1994) *Revolutionary Theatre*. Oxon: Routledge.

Leach, R. (2005) *Revolutionary Theatre*. United Kingdom: Taylor & Francis.

Lucas, A. E. (2020) *Prison Theatre and the Global Crisis of Incarceration*. United Kingdom: Bloomsbury.

Maddox, D. (2023) 'Lee Anderson tells illegal migrants to 'f*** off back to France' if they don't like barges, *The Express*, 8 August. www.express.co.uk/news/politics/1799682/lee-anderson-illegal-migrants-bibby-barge-france.

Mally, L. (2008) 'The Americanization of the Soviet Living Newspaper', *The Carl Beck Papers in Russian and East European Studies* 1903, 1–40.

Matthew, S., and Sellnow, T. (2016) *Narratives of Crisis: Telling Stories of Ruin and Renewal*. Redwood City: Stanford University Press.

Mayhew, S. (2015) *A Dictionary of Geography*. United Kingdom: Oxford University Press.

Mullarkey, R. (2021), 'This Play', in *A Counternarrative: Edition 6*. London: Royal Court Theatre.

Nadler, P. (1995) 'Black Living Newspapers of the Federal Theatre Project', *African American Review* 29(4), 615–22.

Norbury, C. (2020) 'Our World without Open Letter', Creative Industries Federation. https://docs.google.com/document/d/1ZwZTJCb6QKkY0vVx4V67PU4H4bwtW0nGKicsDd1I7vU/edit

Opdycke, S. (2016) *The WPA: Creating Jobs and Hope in the Great Depression*. United States: Taylor & Francis.

Osofisan, F. (2001) *African Theatre: Playwrights & Politics*. Edited by M. Banham, J. Gibbs, and F. Osofisan. Bloomington: Indiana University Press.

Owen, G., O'Brien, D., Taylor, M. (2020). 'A Jobs Crisis in the Cultural and Creative Industries', *Creative Industries: Policy and Evidence Centre*, 10 December. https://pec.ac.uk/blog/how-covid-19-is-impacting-the-cultural-sector-with-the-loss-of-55-000-jobs-in-the-arts.

Plum, J. (1992) 'Rose McClendon and the Black Units of the Federal Theatre Project: A Lost Contribution', *Theatre Survey*, 33(2):144-153

Quinn, S. (2021) *Furious Improvisation: How the WPA and a Cast of Thousands Made High Art Out of Desperate Times*. Lexington, MA: Plunkett Lake Press.

Ravenhill, M., and Shanko, C. (2021) 'Living Newspaper Clippings: Transcript of Mark Ravenhill and Shankho Chaudhuri in Conversation', February, Royal Court Theatre, https://royalcourttheatre.com/living-newspaper-clippings/mark-ravenhill-and-shankho-chaudhuri/.

Raymond, A. (1945) *The Dies Committee: A Study of the Special House Committee for the Investigation of Un-American Activities 1938–1944*. Washington, DC: Catholic University of America Press.

Rich, F. (1986) 'Stage Tale of Apartheid 'Born in the RSA', 3 October, *New York Times*. www.nytimes.com/1986/10/03/theater/stage-tale-of-apartheid-born-in-the-rsa.html.

Roberts, S. (2015) 'The Pioneers', in *The Methuen Drama Guide to Contemporary South African Theatre*, Homann, G., Schnierer, P. P., and Middeke, M., eds., United Kingdom: Bloomsbury, pp. 17–42.

Roitman, J. (2014) *Anti-crisis*. Durham, London: Duke University Press.

Rosenthal, U., and Kouzmin, A. (1993) 'Globalizing an Agenda for Contingencies and Crisis Management: An Editorial Statement', *Journal of Contingencies and Crisis Management*, 1(1), 1–12.

Rosenthal, U., Boin, A., and Comfort, L. K. (2001) *Managing Crises: Threats, Dilemmas, Opportunities*. Springfield, IL: Charles C. Thomas Publisher.

Ross, R. (1974) 'The Role of Blacks in the Federal Theatre, 1935-1939', *The Journal of Negro History* 59(1), 38–50.

Roux-Dufort, C. (2007) 'Is Crisis Management (Only) a Management of Exceptions?', *Journal of Contingencies and Crisis Management*, 15, 105–114.

Royal Court (2020) 5 March, *Royal Court*: 'Royal Court Theatre Announces Open Court: Climate Emergency March 2020, Including the Theatre's Strategy Document for Transitioning to Carbon Net Zero'. https://royalcourttheatre.com/royal-court-theatre-announces-open-court-climate-emergency-march-2020-including-the-theatres-strategy-document-for-transitioning-to-carbon-net-zero/.

Royal Court Theatre (2020a) *Living Newspaper Edition 1*, *Royal Court*, https://royalcourttheatre.com/home/livingnewspaper/living-newpaper-a-counter-narrativeweekly-zine/.

Royal Court Theatre (2020b) Royal Court Theatre to Reopen Doors with New Socially Distanced Live Performance 'Living Newspaper: A Counter Narrative', 14 September, *Royal Court,* https://royalcourttheatre.com/royal-court-theatre-to-reopen-doors-with-new-socially-distanced-live-performance-living-newspaper-a-counter-narrative-in-spaces-around-the-building-from-thursday-12-november-saturday-19-decemb/.

Royal Court Theatre (2020c) 14 September, *Royal Court*. https://d19lfjg8hluhfw.cloudfront.net/wp-content/uploads/2020/09/14131710/Royal-Court-Theatre-Reopening-Announcement-Living-Newspaper.pdf.

Royal Court Theatre (2020d) 30 November *Royal Court*. https://royalcourttheatre.com/writers-announced-for-the-first-edition-of-the-royal-court-theatres-living-newspaper/.

Royal Court Theatre (2021a) 'Living Newspaper Edition 7: The Last Word', *Royal Court*, https://royalcourttheatre.com/whats-on/living-newspaper-edition-7/.

Royal Court Theatre (2021b) 13 April, *Royal Court*. https://royalcourttheatre.com/cast-announced-for-edition-6-of-living-newspaper/.

Samimian-Darash, L., and Rotem, N. (2019) 'From Crisis to Emergency: The Shifting Logic of Preparedness', *Ethnos* 84(5), 910–926.

Senelick, L., and Ostrovsky, S. (2014) *The Soviet Theatre: A Documentary History*. New Haven, Connecticut: Yale University Press.

Simon, B. (1997) *Born in the RSA: Four Workshopped Plays*. Johannesburg: Wits University Press.

Solga, K. (2019) 'Theatre & Performance, Crisis & Survival', *Research in Drama Education* 24(3), 251–6.

Sutton, P. (2005) *The Dramatic Property: A New Paradigm of Applied Theatre Practice for a Globalised Media Culture*. Doctor of Philosophy (PhD) thesis, University of Kent.

Taylor, D, (1991) *Theatre of Crisis: Drama and Politics in Latin America*. USA: University Press of Kentucky.

The Digital, Culture, Media and Sport Committee (2020) 'Impact of COVID-19 on DCMS sectors: First Report', *House of Commons Library*, 23 July 2020. https://committees.parliament.uk/work/250/impact-of-covid19-on-dcms-sectors/publications.

t' Hart, P. (1993) 'Symbols, Rituals and Power: The Lost Dimensions of Crisis Management', *Journal of Contingencies and Crisis Management* 1(1), 36–50.

t' Hart, P. and Boin. A (2001) 'Between Crisis and Normalcy: The Long Shadow of Post-Crisis Politics', in *Managing Crises: Threats, Dilemmas, Opportunities*, U. Rosenthal, A. Boin, and L. K. Comfort eds., Springfield, IL: Charles C. Thomas, pp. 28–46.

Tobin, J. (2020) Covid-19: Impact on the UK Cultural Sector, *House of Lords Library*, 4 September. https://lordslibrary.parliament.uk/covid-19-impact-on-the-uk-cultural-sector/.

Tompkins, J. (2014) *Theatre's Heterotopias: Performance and the Cultural Politics of Space*. United Kingdom: Palgrave Macmillan.

US Congress (1938) 'Investigation of Un-American Propaganda Activities in the United States: Hearings Before a Special Committee on Un-American Activities', House of Representatives, Seventy-fifth Congress, Third Session-Seventy-eighth Congress, Second Session, United States: U.S. Government Printing Office.

Wallace, C. and Escoda, C., Monforte, E., Prado-Pérez, J. R. (2022) *Crisis, Representation and Resilience: Perspectives on Contemporary British Theatre*. London: Bloomsbury.

Walmsley, B., Gilmore, A., O'Brien, D., and Torreggiani, A. (2022) *Culture in Crisis: Impacts of Covid-19 on the UK Cultural Sector and Where We Go from Here*. Leeds: Centre for Cultural Value.

Walsh F. (2010) *Male Trouble: Masculinity and the Performance of Crisis*. London: Palgrave Macmillan.

Wiegand, C. (2020) 3 July, *The Guardian*, www.theguardian.com/stage/2020/jul/03/designers-wrap-uk-theatres-scene-change#:~:text=The%20%23scenechange%20project%20will%20see,their%20usual%20hustle%20and%20bustle.

Witham, B. B. (2003) *The Federal Theatre Project: A Case Study*. Cambridge: Cambridge University Press.

Acknowledgements

The idea for this Element emerged during the UK's first national lockdown as we speculated how performance would endure during and following the COVID-19 pandemic. It has developed substantially since then and our thanks to series editors Liz Tomlin and Trish Reid who saw potential in our initial idea and for ushering this Element from the original proposal to final manuscript.

Thank you to the Royal Court Theatre for providing us with access to recordings of *Living Newspaper: A Counter Narrative* and Lucy Morrison, Jane Fallowfield, and Sam Pritchard for their insightful responses that provided us with a deeper understanding of the making processes involved in creating such an enormous performance event. Our thanks also to Paul Sutton for sharing his experiences and knowledge of C&T.

Thanks to those in the International Federation of Theatre Research Political Performances Working Group who allowed us to test out formative ideas on crisis theatre and offered insightful feedback.

Finally, thanks also to our friends and family for their encouragement and unwavering support during the writing process. Although at times they may have regretted asking what the Element was about or how it was going, they have been invaluable sounding boards and cheerleaders.

Cambridge Elements

Theatre, Performance and the Political

Trish Reid

University of Reading

Trish Reid is Professor of Theatre and Performance and Head of the School of Arts and Communication Design at the University of Reading. She is the author of *The Theatre of Anthony Neilson* (2017), *Theatre & Scotland (2013)*, *Theatre and Performance in Contemporary Scotland* (2024) and co-editor of the *Routledge Companion to Twentieth-Century British Theatre* (2024).

Liz Tomlin

University of Glasgow

Liz Tomlin is Professor of Theatre and Performance at the University of Glasgow. Monographs include *Acts and Apparitions: Discourses on the Real in Performance Practice and Theory* (2013) and *Political Dramaturgies and Theatre Spectatorship: Provocations for Change* (2019). She edited *British Theatre Companies 1995–2014* (2015) and was the writer and co-director with Point Blank Theatre from 1999–2009.

Advisory Board

About the Series

Elements in Theatre, Performance and the Political showcases ground-breaking research that responds urgently and critically to the defining political concerns, and approaches, of our time. International in scope, the series engages with diverse performance histories and intellectual traditions, contesting established histories and providing new critical perspectives.

Cambridge Elements ≡

Theatre, Performance and the Political

Elements in the Series

A full series listing is available at: www.cambridge.org/ETPP

For EU product safety concerns, contact us at Calle de José Abascal, 56–1°, 28003 Madrid, Spain or eugpsr@cambridge.org.

www.ingramcontent.com/pod-product-compliance
Ingram Content Group UK Ltd.
Pitfield, Milton Keynes, MK11 3LW, UK
UKHW022144080726
473066UK00010B/739

* 9 7 8 1 0 0 9 5 2 5 8 1 7 *